IN THE COMPANY OF WRITERS 2005

IN THE COMPANY OF WRITERS 2005

MEADOW BROOK WRITING PROJECT FELLOWS
2005 SUMMER INSTITUTE
OAKLAND UNIVERSITY

Weekly Reader Press
New York Lincoln Shanghai

In the Company of Writers 2005

Copyright © 2007 by Ron Sudol

All rights reserved. No part of this book may be used or reproduced by any means, graphic, electronic, or mechanical, including photocopying, recording, taping or by any information storage retrieval system without the written permission of the publisher except in the case of brief quotations embodied in critical articles and reviews.

Weekly Reader Press
an imprint of iUniverse, Inc.
and the Weekly Reader Corporation

iUniverse books may be ordered through booksellers or by contacting:

iUniverse
2021 Pine Lake Road, Suite 100
Lincoln, NE 68512
www.iuniverse.com
1-800-Authors (1-800-288-4677)

Because of the dynamic nature of the Internet, any Web addresses or links contained in this book may have changed since publication and may no longer be valid.

The views expressed in this work are solely those of the author and do not necessarily reflect the views of the publisher, and the publisher hereby disclaims any responsibility for them.

Credit for Graphics: Dover Pictorial Archives Electronic Clip Art Series, Dover Publications, Inc.

ISBN: 978-0-595-46792-1 (pbk)

Printed in the United States of America

Contents

Foreword		ix
Chapter 1	Michelle Ballard	1
Chapter 2	Felecia Branch	13
Chapter 3	Dwayne L. Brown	17
Chapter 4	John Callaghan	21
Chapter 5	Carolyn Carrington	33
Chapter 6	Mary Cox	37
Chapter 7	Ahna Felix-Brown	41
Chapter 8	Catherine Haar	57
Chapter 9	Kathy Hribar	61
Chapter 10	Liz Kozek	71
Chapter 11	Lois Little	79
Chapter 12	Herman A. Peterson	85
Chapter 13	Kathleen Reddy-Butkovich	99
Chapter 14	Stacy Tines	103

Acknowledgments

We would like to thank Professor Ron Sudol, director of the Meadow Brook Writing Project, for his steadfast leadership and vision. We are also grateful to co-directors Mary Cox, Kathleen Reddy-Butkovich, and John Callaghan, who facilitated the Summer Institute. Their constant encouragement and inspiration created an atmosphere of collaboration that allowed writing to flourish. The 2005 Writing Project Fellows immersed themselves in this collaborative atmosphere, sharing their ideas and helping to shape each other's work. Through the willingness of Fellows to open themselves to the creative process, these writings have grown into much more than what each author might have produced on their own. Finally, we owe thanks to Oakland University liaisons Catherine Haar and Kathleen Lawson for help and guidance in the publishing and editing processes. With their help, this book has become a reality.

Foreword

The teachers of writing are writers. Why is this statement not as obvious as "The teachers of dentistry are dentists," or "The teachers of nursing are nurses"?

Writing is a craft, and the Meadow Brook Writing Project exists to connect the craft with those who teach it from kindergarten through college. So we were told on the very first day of the MBWP Summer Institute at Oakland University in the summer of 2005. But we were told this only AFTER we had written something. On that very first day, we were required to write about our names, and the reading of our writing served as a class introduction. We wrote every day of our Summer Institute after that as well. The best of that writing–poetry, drama, fiction, and nonfiction–is contained in this 2005 volume of *In the Company of Writers*.

In addition to our names, some of our writing turned out to be autobiographical as well, if not in fact, then at least in fiction, in the processes of making meaning and exploring personal issues. This kind of writing naturally led to writing about our families. You will find stories about our spouses, parents, children, and grandparents. Many of us consider our pets to be part of the family as well, and writing about animals blossomed into writing about nature in general. Our professional lives were not spared the scrutiny of our pens, naturally. We wrote about teaching and learning, from both the teacher's point of view and the student's point of view. On the very last day of the 2005 Meadow Brook Writing Project Summer Institute, we the fellows (although exhausted at this point) were asked to write a class song. We came up with lyrics that go along nicely to the tune of "My Bonnie Lies Over the Ocean." The most memorable and significant part was the first line of our refrain:

"The teachers of writing are writers."

The point had been driven home. What follows is an eclectic compilation of writings from teachers of writing. If you enjoy reading it half as much as we have enjoyed writing it, then our summer of continuing education was a success.

—*Herman A. Peterson and Kathy Hribar, Editors*

Chapter 1

Michelle Ballard

The Kindergartner in Me!!!
(From the point of view of a five year-old)

Adventurous, Bubbling, Daring–
The Kindergartner in Me!

Singing, Twisting, Tumbling–
The Kindergartner in Me!

Energetic, Intelligent, Independent–
The Kindergartner in Me!

Thumb-Sucking, Noise Making, Even Surprising–
The Kindergartner in Me!

Sponge-Bob-Lover, Hot Wheels Collector, Legos Builder too–
The Kindergartner in Me!

Messy, Curious, Never in my seat–
The Kindergartner in Me!

Helper, Leader, Eloquent Speaker–
The Kindergartner in Me!

It's not hard to love me, when you understand–
The Kindergartner in Me!

Beginning Kindergarten:
A Play from the Teacher's Point of View

Dramatis Personae:

Mrs. Carol, Kindergarten Teacher
Mrs. Karen, Teacher's Aide
Mrs. Johnson, School Principal
Tony, School Custodian
Mrs. Smith, School Secretary
Parent One
Jamie, a helpful six year-old student
Thomas, an active four year-old student
Sarah, a joyful five year-old student
Brian, a five year-old student
Parent Two
Parent Three
Other students and parents

Scene One:

[Inside a kindergarten classroom. A few neatly piled boxes, covered bookshelves, etc., show that school is not yet in session.]

[Enter Mrs. Carol and Mrs. Karen carrying yet more boxes.]

Mrs. Carol: Mrs. Karen, it's about 2:00. We've got all day tomorrow to put finishing touches on things to get ready for the new school year, so let's cut out early today. Tomorrow we can find a place for everything and put everything in its place, as I like to say.

[Enter Mrs. Johnson.]
Mrs. Johnson: *[in a pleasant manner]* Oh, I'm so glad I caught you before you left for the day.

Mrs. Carol: Hello, Mrs. Johnson. Do you really need both of us? I've worked Mrs. Karen hard for two weeks, and I promised her she could leave early today.

Mrs. Johnson: *[pleasantly]* No, I don't have a problem with that. We will see you tomorrow, Mrs. Karen. *[Exit Mrs. Karen.]* Carol, let's sit and talk for a moment.

Mrs. Carol: *[concerned]* Okay, sure.

Mrs. Johnson: *[looking around the room, surprised]* Oh my, you have really outdone yourself this year. I feel as if I've walked into Dr. Seuss Land. Girl, Universal Studios has nothing on you! These are the cutest Dr. Seuss name tags. And look at these fifteen little Dr. Seuss hats hanging in the reading center, one for each student. I love the Seuss alphabet chart and these smocks and curtains. You must have spent your whole summer putting this together.

Mrs. Carol: Oh, please. This is nothing. You know I decorate my room in a theme each year.

Mrs. Johnson: *[pausing]* Yes, I do, and after seeing this, I really feel bad about what I have to tell you.

Mrs. Carol: Well, go ahead. I see some blue Legos in the red bucket and I'm just going to step over here and straighten this out while we talk.

Mrs. Johnson: *[reserved]* No, I think you better sit down for this. *[waiting for her to take a seat]* I just heard from my supervisor that due to School Board budget cuts we can only have one kindergarten class, so Ms. Little will not be returning to our school this year.

Mrs. Carol: *[taking a long deep breath and standing to her feet]* Does that mean I will have 30 students this year instead of the 15 I was promised?

Mrs. Johnson: *[motioning for Carol to sit down, speaking softly but firmly]* Yes, it does, and that's not all.

Mrs. Carol: *[snapping a bit, but remaining professional]* Not all! Well, what's the rest? Are they taking my aide too?

Mrs. Johnson: *[calmly]* No, they're not taking your aide. But this wing of the building uses an awful lot of heat and air conditioning, and since there is only one class in this wing now, they have asked me to move you to another wing of the building so they can shut this wing down for the year.

Mrs. Carol: *[with an exasperated look on her face]* Are they out of their minds? I have given the School Board twenty-eight long years and this is what they do to me two days—*[stops to look at her watch]* well, it's almost 3:00 now—so a day before school starts? I have been teaching kindergarten in this room for over 15 years now. How am I supposed to move it all in one day? *[placing hands in the air showing disgust]* As my children would say, "What's with that?"

Mrs. Johnson: *[with an understanding tone]* I hear you. But, we have been through worse than this. I know you can make it work. I'll have my secretary bring down your new class list first thing in the morning, and I'll send the new custodian to help you get everything moved and ready for the first day. Go home and relax. Deal with this tomorrow.

Mrs. Carol: *[grabbing her purse and speaking sarcastically]* Yeah, just call me Wonder Woman. I can do everything it took me to do in two weeks ... in one day. Oh, yeah ... sure ... no problem.

Mrs. Johnson: *[turning to console Carol]* At least you have a job. I've got to call pregnant Ms. Little and tell her she doesn't have a teaching position. Remember, we've just got to follow the cheese.

Mrs. Carol: No offense, but the cheese just melted. I'll see you tomorrow.

[Exit Mrs. Carol followed slowly by Mrs. Johnson.]

<u>Scene Two:</u>

[Inside a different classroom. Everything is ready, except for a few empty boxes piled near the door.]

[Enter Mrs. Carol and Mrs. Karen.]

Mrs. Carol: *[wiping her brow]* Okay, Karen, we've been here since 8:00 this morning and it is now 7:00 p.m. I'm just going to make sure I've got the basics for tomorrow set and then we can go home. The little ones will be here tomorrow. I can't believe I have to throw away these fifteen beautiful Dr. Seuss nametags. Since I'll have 30 students, I'll just have to use these basic apple nametags from the teacher store.

[Enter Tony dragging curtains. Hearing footsteps, Mrs. Carol looks at the door. She speaks with a panicked voice to Tony.]

Are those my Dr. Seuss curtains that I sewed together by hand that you are dragging on the floor? *[calming down, flipping her hands in the air]* But, you know what? At this point it doesn't really matter, because we've gone from "Welcome to Dr. Seuss Land" to "Basic Letters, Shapes and Color World." Just throw the curtains away.

Mrs. Karen: *[walking toward the custodian and speaking to teacher]* Carol, come on. Don't get sidetracked. Finish your plans for the day. I'll fold these curtains carefully and put them in a box, and you can deal with them later. *[Shooing the custodian away, she puts the curtains away. Exit Tony.]* Look, we've been here a very long time anyway. You're just tired. Tomorrow is the first day of school and the little ones will only be here for 2 ½ hours. We can make it through that.

Mrs. Carol: You're right, Karen. This is just not the way I like things done. Yes, it is time to go. Hand me my purse out of the closet. Do you need a ride?

Mrs. Karen: No, I drove today. Thanks anyway.

[Exit Mrs. Karen and Mrs. Carol.]

<u>Scene Three:</u>

[The same classroom, now very neat.]

[Enter Mrs. Karen and Mrs. Carol, who stand just inside the door. Enter students and parents.]

Mrs. Carol: Come on in, boys and girls, and choose a toy to play with from the toy center. *[She turns to address a group of parents.]* Welcome to kindergarten. Go have a cup of coffee and we will see you back here at 11:25.

[Exit parents.]

Mrs. Smith: *[calling from the office P.A. system]* Mrs. Carol?

Mrs. Carol: *[answering P.A. system]* Yes?

Mrs. Smith: *[speaking from P.A. system]* Mrs. Johnson needs Mrs. Karen to assist with registration in the large gym.

Mrs. Carol: *[waving to Mrs. Karen, speaking to the P.A. system]* Sure, she's on her way.

Mrs. Karen: Hopefully, they won't need me all morning.

Mrs. Carol: *[trying to be pleasant]* Just go, and hurry back.

[Exit Mrs. Karen. Enter Parent One.]

Parent One: Hi, Mrs. Carol. I was hoping I could stay and videotape Brittany's first day of school for her dad, who is fighting in Iraq.

[Before Mrs. Carol can respond …]

Jamie: *[coming over and continuously tapping Mrs. Carol on her hip]* Teacher, Teacher, Teacher!

Mrs. Carol: *[ignoring Jamie, responds to parent]* According to administration policy, I'm not supposed to allow such. But, since he is defending our country, I don't see why I can't make an exception this once.

[Suddenly a huge thud comes from the library center. Mrs. Carol stands with a shocked look on her face and her mouth wide open.]

Jamie: *[tugging Mrs. Carol's skirt]* That's what I was trying to tell you. Brian was messing with the books in the book area, and he won't let me see *Green Eggs and Ham*.

Mrs. Carol: *[trying to keep her composure, talking to Jamie and the class]* You guys were told to play in the toy area. Okay, boys and girls, put the toys away while Brian and I pick up all the books. Then join me on the carpet for circle time.

[While putting the toys away, Thomas begins singing the Barney "Clean-up" song and dunking the toys in the toy buckets. The other students follow suit.]

Mrs. Carol: *[not happy]* Boys and girls, it is not song time, and, Thomas, we don't throw toys. Come and sit on the carpet. *[motioning for all the children to sit on the carpet]* Boys and girls, we are going to read one of my favorite books, but before we do that … let's go over the rules. *[pointing to the rule poster]* Repeat after me … Everyone must wait for his or her turn quietly.

Class: Everyone must wait for their turn quietly.

Mrs. Carol: There is a time and a place for every activity.

Class: There is a time and a place for every activity.

Mrs. Carol: There is a place for everything …

Class: There is a place for everything …

Mrs. Carol: And everything must be in its place.

Class: And everything must be in its place.

Mrs. Carol: You must ask permission to use the bathroom.

Class: You must ask permission to use the bathroom.

Mrs. Carol: You must raise your hand if you wish to speak.

Class: You must raise you hand if you wish to speak.

Mrs. Carol: *[picking up the story book]* Our story for today is *Chicka Chicka*

Thomas: *[cutting off Mrs. Carol and leaping into the sky, yelling]* Boom! Boom! My mom has that book at home.

Sarah: *[joining Thomas' excitement]* Yeah, me too!

Thomas and Sarah: *[simultaneously, with a jazzy rhythm]* A told B and B told C …

Mrs. Carol: *[sternly interrupting them and pointing towards the rules]* Thomas and Sarah, it is not your turn. Sit down quietly and listen to the story. *[looking at the clock]* Oh my, I'm afraid our story will have to wait. It is time for us—quietly—to walk and tour the building.

Thomas: *[yelling out with a one-arm gesture]* Yes!

Mrs. Carol: *[pointing sternly]* Quietly, Thomas. *[Aside.]* I could really use Karen to help me with this. *[lining up the students]* When I call the first letter of your name, line up at the door. If the first letter in your name begins with C ... line up. *[watching the students line up]* Good job. Now, if your name begins with T ...

Thomas: *[running to the door]* Chicka, Chicka, Boom Boom ...

Mrs. Carol: *[annoyed]* Thomas, come back and line up quietly. Now the next letter is B ... *[Mrs. Carol sees that Brian does not move. She walks over to Brian and whispers to him.)* Your name begins with B ... so you can line up now. *[Brian does not move.]* Brian, is there a problem?

Brian: *[putting his head down in his lap]* I want my mommy! *[He begins to cry.]*

Mrs. Carol: *[gently lifting Brian by his arm]* Brian, you'll see her soon. Come go with us for now. *[noticing the puddle on the floor—becoming annoyed again]* Brian, you've had an accident. We talked about the rules for the bathroom. Why didn't you just ask to go?

Brian: *[Brian starts crying louder and louder as he shouts.]* I want my Mommy! I want my Mommy!

Mrs. Carol: *[Aside.]* I don't believe this. How long are they going to keep Karen? *[in a normal tone]* Brian, calm down. The office will handle it. Who knows where the office is?

Jamie: *[raising her hand and speaking]* I know where it is. I can take him.

Mrs. Carol: *[with a sigh of relief]* Good, okay, Jamie, take Brian to the office, and he can wait there for his mom.

Mrs. Carol: *[looking at her watch]* Boys and girls, we are a bit off schedule, but we'll catch up. Okay, I'd like those girls and boys who are still sitting on the carpet to join the line for the school tour.

[Line of students with Mrs. Carol at the head exit stage right, then shortly enter stage left.]

Mrs. Carol: Boys and girls, we have finished our tour, and you all have done a great job walking in the hall. Now, I have a special art sheet for each of you from our story, *Chicka Chicka Boom Boom*. *[After she has passed out the art sheets, she has one left over and notices that a student is missing. She looks around frantically.]*

[Enter Mrs. Karen with a student who is crying.]

Mrs. Karen: *[talking to Mrs. Carol]* Look who I found!

Mrs. Carol: *[hugging the student]* I'm so glad to see you. I've got a special art sheet just for you. *[looking at the clock]* Boys and girls, it is time to clean up and be dismissed.

[Everyone helps to tidy the room, and then the students line up.]

Mrs. Carol: Boys and girls, when you see your parent come to the door, let me know.

Parent One: *[talking to Mrs. Carol]* Thanks for allowing me to stay.

Mrs. Carol: Oh, you're welcome. *[giving a big hug to Brittany]* See you tomorrow.

[Parents begin to enter randomly.]

Parent Two: Hi, Mrs. Carol, I'm looking, but I don't see Brian.

Mrs. Carol: Brian is in the office. Nobody called you?

Parent Two: *[sounding alarmed]* No, what happened?

Mrs. Carol: *[with a clipboard in her hand]* Brian had a difficult day. I'm not sure he's ready for kindergarten. He started out being in an area he was not supposed to be in, and caused an entire bookshelf to fall down. When I asked him to line up for our tour of the school, he refused and that really held us up. Then I noticed he had soiled himself, and he just started crying, "I want my mommy!" He just seems to be rather immature for this class. We have bathrooms right inside our class, and there is no reason for those types of mistakes to happen. *(gesturing toward the office)* You and your husband should talk about it. This might not be the placement for him right now.

Thomas: *[Seeing his mom approach the door with balloons that say "I'm proud of you," he runs toward the door and leaps into her arms, yelling excitedly]* Mommy, Mommy, Mommy!

Mrs. Carol: *[frustrated with his behavior, sternly stating]* Thomas, you get back in that line! You are to tell me your mom is here! *[Thomas drops his head and returns to the line. Mrs. Carol turns to talk to his mom]* Is he always like this? He may need a behavior modification program!

Parent Three: *[shocked]* What did he do?

Mrs. Carol: *[looking at clipboard]* Where do I begin? He was singing in class, throwing toys, running to get in line, yelling out and just constantly disrupting the day.

Parent Three: *[disappointed in teacher and son]* Well, he's only four, and he was so excited about being in school. He's been in a Nurture Care center for two years with, at the most, seven kids.

Mrs. Carol: *[not backing down]* Well, I've got thirty four-, five-, and six-year-olds in this room, and he is going to have to calm down.

Parent Three: *[snatching Thomas]* Come on here! What were you doing in that room today? Mommy's gonna burst each of these balloons right now! (*Thomas is crying because he disappointed his mom. Parent Three exits frustrated and disappointed.*)

Mrs. Carol: *[talking to Karen with an exhausted tone]* Well, everyone's been picked up. I can't believe this day. If this is any indication of the rest of the year, I think I'm going to consider early retirement.

[Exit Mrs. Carol and Mrs. Karen.]

FINIS.

My Name

When I think of my name, I always associate it with being common—nothing special at all. You see, teachers, students, neighbors and even strangers could always pronounce my name with no trouble. Many times I found myself in the company of at least one other little girl bearing the same name. Whether at church, playing in the park, or shopping in the mall, you could hear the sounds of various moms calling, "Michelle!" "Michelle!" "Michelle!" as three different little girls would turn their heads. I learned at an early age if I were going to be memorable and unique it would be because of the content of my character, not the character of my name. What is it that makes me unique? It is my

> Meticulous and sincere demeanor with
> Intuitive and dedicated characteristics, as I
> Carefully caress each experience with
> Hardwork,
> Energy,
> Love and loyalty.
> Leaving
> Everyone with a lasting memory of myself.

Chapter 2

Felecia Branch

What's in a Name?

A description, a definition, a defining of who you are, yes and no, it depends on the person. Greetings, Salutations, Felicitations, my name is Felecia, named so by my mother. She named me after the famous and beautiful 1960's movie star, Felicia Farr. In Latin, my name is Felicity, which means "happiness."

I believe I fit my name. It is a perfect complement to me. Overall, I am a generally happy person. My aura permeates like a bright shining star, reminiscent of the color-wash of autumn leaves.

Serious, silly, funny, corny at times, a lover of learning. I am Felecia.

Peace.

My Personal Journey

There are certain moments in life that can place your world as you know it into a total upheaval. An upheaval not only of what you have treasured, valued, and believed, but an upheaval to crush your faith in man, and possibly your faith in God. A situation where you are truly at an impasse, where you have been knocked down and counted out for all intents and purposes, never to rise again. The past two years of my life had been this way; wracked with trauma, turmoil, trials, and seemingly unlimited tribulations that have ripped my very soul. Betrayal, mistrust, divorce, denial, depression–sinking, slimy reservoirs where everything drags you deeper and deeper into a bottomless dark, dank, abysmal pit. Yet, through the fog and mire, clarity comes, little by little, inching its way along, attaching itself like vines to your soul, anchoring you and heralding a new day, whispering to you that all is not lost.

Arise from the ash heap that you thought was your life, and gaze upon a new day. A day that, if you surrender it to your loss and your depression and your disappointment, you will never fully claim.

Before the final count was listed, I had indeed pulled myself up from the ashheap and embarked upon my journey back to "me." I slowly began to find myself. I say "find" because I had lost myself totally. However, through my journey I've learned, and am learning still, not only to find me, but to "champion" my own cause for change. To reclaim myself, and never to betray myself, to not doubt or question my feelings, instincts, talents, attractiveness, or my abilities. At the very moment that I ceased to try and push the river, my world began moving again. God and the universe ordered, or reordered, my path and continue to do so. I saw my life realigning itself and following its own divinely set pace; at times rushing, pushing, slowly creeping, yet always steadily traveling over the terrains of my life–forever pushing me to go forward.

Is this a lesson easily learned? NOOOO!!! But, it is a lesson that can only be understood by facing life–by putting on your boxing gloves and boldly entering the arena, by withstanding the battering blows belting your bruised body. And finally realizing that after each round of assault you've survived, that your hard won victory is not based on any man's final score or tally, but is earned by just simply hanging in there. If strength is born of endurance, then peace must be a by-product of intense suffering. Therefore, dare greatly, dream new dreams, fight boldly, love deeply, forgive freely, make new memories, relinquish regrets and remorse, and eagerly anticipate a new day with beautiful beginnings.

A Conversation with My Son

The day started off as any other; it was hot, humid, and muggy. I arose at 5:30 a.m. to get myself ready for the day. At 6:30 I awoke my son, Justin, and began getting him ready for day camp. I made his favorite breakfast–French toast–packed up the car, and proceeded to drop him at camp. Later on that evening, around 7:00, his dad arrived to pick him up for his parenting time visit. At 9:20 p.m. I heard his truck pull into the driveway; Justin jumped out and rang the doorbell. I was glad because I had missed him when he was gone. As the evening progressed, we played two quick games of pick-up sticks. After he had beaten me horribly in both games he said, "Mommy." I responded, "Yes." "Why do things keep changing for us?" he said.

I thought a moment before asking, "Do you mean the fact that your dad and I are living in separate houses?" I reply. "Yes," he said. "I don't like it, it's too much. My little heart is breaking. I wish I had never been born, then I wouldn't have to go through this." At this moment my own heart is breaking. It is breaking for all the hurt, pain, and confusion that I know my little boy feels. "God please help me," I say to myself.

"Sweetheart, if you were never born then my life would not be worth living, for what would I ever do without you? I know that things are different now and there has been a lot of change, but I promise you, even though you can't imagine it, things are going to be OK. And I know that because GOD himself has told me so. And I want you to always remember that mommy loves you and will be here for you." My son continued to cry late into the night, a sad wrenching cry that lasted until he eventually fell asleep in my arms. I lay there looking at him sleep, thinking how much I wished I could take his pain away. How can you ever explain to your six year old child why their world has fallen apart? How can you adequately tell him or her that mommy and daddy are getting divorced and make it OK for them? The answer is: you can't.

If I could take his pain and bear it myself, I gladly would, without hesitation. My challenge is to love him deeply and reassure him that although our family is no longer together, everyone still loves him, and that that is never going to change. But I also want him to know that change is an inevitable and necessary part of life; that it is the only real constant in the universe. And that without change many wonderful things would never happen, like the barren trees in winter blooming in the spring, the caterpillar transforming into the beautiful butterfly, the small kernel of wheat that enters the ground and dies only to rise again in multiplied magnificence, or the cycle of all life continuing through death, birth and rebirth: a never-ending cycle of change. I want him to know that by keeping GOD first in our lives, all is going to be OK and that the universe will unfold as it should.

And lastly, I want him to know that above and beyond all these things, that I have already claimed our victory: the victory of my son being a happy, healthy, loving, well-adjusted young man—one who will be all that I want him to be, yet far, far more than I can ever imagine or anticipate. I have learned to find the lesson in my trial because there is always something there to learn. One need only be still and listen for the voice of GOD. I will carry my son on his journey as GOD has carried me; and over time he, too will learn that with faith, perseverance, and love that each dawn will herald a beautiful new day.

Chapter 3

Dwayne L. Brown

Uncle Earnest

My Uncle Earnest will be 89 years old. I do not know his birthday; I guess I never did. He was never one for celebrating that kind of thing. He is a quiet gentle giant. I have always admired his work ethic (a lot like my dad). In fact most summers as a youth were shared under his watch. I worked for my uncle along with my cousins (his two boys, Ken and Den) sorting out store hooks. I never knew what those hooks were until, as an adult, I happened to notice them adorning a pegboard in a hardware store. And that is where the epiphany for me collapsed.

Along the makeshift shelves, the hooks hung a range of products. "Those damn hooks!" I exclaimed in that nostalgic monotone voice, as if I were still that same devious lad seeking that fearful sound of that 70's discipline "Boy-what-you-say" reprimand of my boyhood days. There they were, the hooks, altogether just as strong and enduring as my beloved Uncle Earnest. Never noticed but needed for security. Like a cog in a wheel doing the one thing to keep the big wheels "a turning."

It was hard to see this statue of a man now confined to a wheelchair. He had truly played out his role as uncle, a role that I never measured up to with my own nephew. It seems that when I reflect on just my childhood experiences there was

Uncle Earnest—just like them hooks. I could not appreciate him then, but I rejoice in him now.

Oh, the places I have been with Uncle Earnest! First and foremost with him, it was off to church were he was the greatest deacon I have ever known. From there we traveled to countless sporting events from baseball games at Mansfield Park (over and around by Conner somewhere by Mack off of Shoemaker). I remember it being close to home. Then, "Welcome to the main event." Wrestling. Oh, yes, I used to be somewhat of a fanatic when wrestling was as real as the fire being thrown into the ring. This all took place down at Cobo Hall Arena. Uncle Earnest took us to see the Thunderbirds, my favorite Roller Derby team at the Olympia Stadium on Grand River. Now there's a sport you don't have to worry about a salary cap for anymore!

But of all those great sporting events, my favorite was not the professional or Minor League games or athletic events; it was quite simply the laymen of Firemen Field Day at old Tiger Stadium. I wonder where they are holding it today?

Where are the hooks?

I digress, as if I could fit in the back of that green station wagon and head down South once again. Thanks to Uncle Earnest as the pilot and Auntie as the co-pilot, we navigated way back to Allendale, South Carolina, where not only did we visit my maternal side of the family, we also spent 50 percent of the stay with my Uncle Earnest's people, down the road a ways on Highway 3. Man, that's where I got my love for hot-warm chicken in aluminum foil; it was Auntie's. But her cooking is another story. That was all that was needed for the entire journey, along with my cousins, and Uncle Earnest.

Somewhere around the late 80's my uncle suffered from a ... I don't know what happened. All I know is this: he fell from the stairs leading down from the back door. Together, he and I must have climbed those stairs a million times. It became painfully apparent that his fall would be his one-millionth and last attempt. The fall left him bound to a wheelchair. Bound but always determined. I have seen my uncle play his role as father of the grooms and brides at all of his children's weddings. Both Linda and Michelle were stunningly gorgeous brides with their dad by their sides. His union with the wheelchair did not stop him from fulfilling his fatherly duties. He would also, still, from time to time, put a good old fashion whooping on my pop in card games like Bid Whist and Spades. Lord knows, my dad needed to be whopped.

Uncle Earnest's condition worsened, and he became more and more the convalescent; but, you know, his voice never changed. He always had a matter-of-fact tone of voice, and I consider Uncle Earnest to be my first professor. So when I saw him for the first time lying in the hospital bed, both legs amputated, and when my Aunt asked him in the way she does the "Reagan" ritual, "Earnest, who is that?!" my uncle, alert, almost cursed and said, "Ah, shoot. That's Dwayne."

I could not ask him for a story in its entirety, so I settled for the hook. Even though Uncle Earnest married into the family like Uncle Sammy, they get the same amount of love and respect as my blood uncles, like my favorite late Uncle Robert. All of these uncles are on my mother's side of the family.

Here's to you, Uncle Earnest. Thanks for being a real uncle and a role model, for living, not just playing the role. You hooked me up and I love you.

Chapter 4

John Callaghan

Sacred Secrets

My dinner partner was laughing. "Why do you look so shocked?" The amusement in his voice cut through the sounds of the various customers eating dinner at the Colonial Restaurant.

"C'mon, you say you were in China that year? 1949? That was 11 or 12 years ago, the year the communists took over the whole country!" I couldn't keep the tinges of wonder and doubt out of my voice.

"Exactly."

"Exactly? How could an American be in China in 1949 and survive?"

"They didn't take me for an American."

"From what I've read, no one could get in there. What made you an exception?"

"Parachute."

"C'mon … you're pullin' my chain. That's James Bond stuff."

"Sometimes we actually did what you read in those books."

"'We'? Who are 'we'?"

"CIA. I was one of their original recruits, early 1947."

"You were a spy in China?"

"For two years I was everything from, you name it, a grunt in the Chinese Army, a rice paddy peasant, a factory laborer—it all depended on circumstances."

My mind whirled with confusion as I tried to focus on his words. The triangular asceticism of the face didn't match the words. The casual remark about him being in China stunned me. The normal sounds of the other diners, the hum of male and female voices, the clinking of glass and silverware, all made the whole thing even more incongruous to me.

I could still remember the way the guy looked on the first day of class, sitting near the door up front, somewhat separate from most of the students, pen poised over notebook, listening to Professor Hirten's explication of the course and assignments. His clothing was neat, casual. He had introduced himself to the class as Doug Marshall but, even then, something about him made him seem different from the others, at least to me. It wasn't just the way he sat or had positioned himself, or even the fact that it was a night class, a graduate course in Modern American Poetry. Maybe it had to do with my circumstances. I had gotten special permission from the dean to take the class as my final 3 credits in literature to qualify for my BA so most of the people in the class were graduate students, older than I and a lot more experienced.

But I don't think it was age or experience that made the man different. He had a healthy glow about him, his body language serene, a sense of complete self-confidence, an aura no one else in that room had. Yet he never dominated any of the discussions, some of them quite heated, of Dickinson, Whitman, Frost. He read selections and gave his opinion when asked; he obviously knew his stuff but he never imposed any of his ideas on anyone.

Until after midterm exams in late March. The class had been discussing the nature images Frost used in his poems and what they were supposed to mean. I volunteered to analyze "West Running Brook," a favorite of mine: how the movement of the water was a symbol of the flow of life and that all that energy was heading toward a traditional symbol of death—the West where the sun set and 'died.' Professor Hirten, as usual, smiled and nodded as other students gave their interpretations of some of Frost's other poems.

At the break I was out in the smoking area sucking on a Pall Mall. I was surprised to see Doug Marshall standing next to me, telling me he thought Frost was over-interpreted and in some ways over-rated. His words were casual, conversational, but I couldn't help feeling the guy was more than politely disagreeing with my interpretation of poetry.

I looked into those dark brown eyes, some how enigmatic and amused all at the same time.

"You sound more like a teacher than a student."

"Probably because I am."

"Well, that makes sense. Where do you teach?"

"Saint Michael's Seminary."

"Oh. When I was in the seminary, all my teachers were priests."

"Now you're two for two."

"You're a priest? I guess I shouldn't be surprised, but I am."

"I dress casual for class. It causes fewer distractions."

"Well, those future priests you teach need good English teachers. I had some pretty good ones myself, especially in high school. I have a feeling you're a good one too."

"Thanks. It's ironic but I didn't come out here to tease you. I like your attitude about things. And maybe find out if you've ever thought about the seminary, about the priesthood. But now I find you've already done that."

"Sacred Heart Seminary. Detroit. I left on good terms with them. I was impatient. The funny thing is I have no idea what I'll do when I graduate in June. Right now I'm so busy with an overload of classes, working a job and playing lacrosse I haven't had time to think about what happens after June."

"I know what that's like even though for me it was almost 20 years ago. I did my undergraduate work at Catholic U. in Washington. It's amazing how much my last semester was like yours: extra classes, job and baseball, not lacrosse. And I wasn't sure what I was going to do either."

"Interesting. So you were an English major too."

"No. Foreign languages. I was thinking about working overseas."

"What happened?"

"Well, I did for awhile. But I kept coming back to the vocation idea, to becoming a priest. Couldn't shake it. And here I am working on a Master's in English so I can be a qualified literature teacher of future priests."

"Why not teach foreign languages?"

"We don't teach oriental languages."

"You majored in *oriental* languages?"

"Yep. Look, we got to get back to class. I don't have Confessions this Saturday. How about dinner at the Colonial? I'm buying. Maybe we can talk a little about what happens to you after June."

"You're on. I gotta work to 6:30 so I can't get there 'til 7:00, 7:30."

"That's fine. See you there."

So there we were sitting in a booth at the Colonial, the dinner conversations rising and falling around us, the odors of various fish dinners and cheesy pastas wafting about us, and I was amazed at what I was hearing.

"How could they take you for Chinese … you don't *look* Chinese."

"You'd be surprised how easy it was. It didn't take much. I spoke the language, even some of the dialects. There are more mixed breeds in China than people realize, especially those of Russian blood. And they were always surprised I was American."

"You got caught?"

"Oh, no. I wouldn't be here if that happened. The authorities never knew. But when I made contact with the underground elements, they were always shocked, especially the priests."

"I thought they shot all the priests or put them in prison."

"Not all. Many of them went along with the public atheism; some of them even went through a kind of public defrocking ceremony. But they said Mass and administered the sacraments in secret. I usually found out about who and where they were, especially if I was a laborer on one of the farms or a factory worker in the city."

"What did they think of having an American Catholic, uh, spy in their midst? They must have loved making contact with someone like you."

"Not at all. One night I went to confession to an underground priest and he was outraged. After absolution he stalked off and refused to speak to me."

"That doesn't make sense."

"Anyone who was not one of them was an enemy, not just the communists. Eventually, I had to move to another area because I couldn't trust him."

"I can't believe I'm sitting here talking to a priest who was a spy. I thought I was going to dinner with a guy in my poetry class who happened to be a priest."

"That's true, but there's more to it than just that."

I tried to focus my attention on the conversation, but my feelings were becoming more and more ambivalent. Who was this guy really? A priest? OK. A student and teacher of English? Yes. But an ex-spy? It was hard to accept. It certainly did not match my image of what a spy was–someone lurking in the shadows with a license to kill, someone who made people believe he was something he was not.

"What are you thinking, Sean?" The voice was quiet, sincere, the eyes amused.

"I'm thinking you don't fit the image of a spy. You know, a trained killer, someone who secretly blows things up—I dunno, someone who seduces beautiful women and extracts secrets from them. Certainly not someone who would become a priest. How did that happen, anyway?"

The smile was genuine, but the eyes had a touch of sadness to them.

"It began when my de-briefer suggested I apply my-uh-'high sense of morality'-to social work or teaching."

"Your de-briefer? What's that?"

"A who. He was my controller, my boss. When I quit, it was his job to make sure I was sincere and to let me know what I could and couldn't do after I was out."

"You quit ... I thought you couldn't quit once you were in."

"That's definitely truer now than back in those days. You have to remember the Agency was very new then. They recruited guys like me-idealistic, unattached; they did extensive background checks, even interviewed my high school teachers. We trained for over a year-very physical, very intense-they tested us for everything, especially loyalty to flag and country."

"A lot of gung-ho stuff?"

"In a way. But we were already enthusiastic, you might say 'patriotic.' Remember, we were students in Washington who were involved in politics and campaigns all throughout our college years there. You know, working for senators or congressmen, especially in the summer. The emphasis in our training was on the communist intent to undermine and replace democratic systems and how they planned to do it."

"Did you find that to be true in China?"

"Absolutely. I saw it first hand every day I was there. That's another reason so many of the ordinary people trusted no one—they were confused. They knew the communist propaganda and the reality of their lives didn't match up at all, but Western ways were foreign to them too, totally different from the subsistence farming that was a way of life for the majority of them for centuries. Some of them cooperated with us only because they saw us as the lesser of two evils."

"Why did you quit, then?"

"I got very uncomfortable with some of my assignments. At first my bosses were pleased with the information I got for them. But I began to realize the information would be used against some of the people I befriended or at least make them suspect to the authorities.

"My boss told me not to worry about how the information got used, that how they used the info wasn't my decision anyway."

"They weren't happy with your work?"

"Oh, no. Their attitude was, 'Oh, you have a moral problem with this? An issue of ethics? Don't worry; we'll never ask you to do anything you consider immoral.' But I could tell they would prefer I did more than get information for them."

"What more could you have done?"

Fr. Marshall paused, frowning with concentration or, perhaps, reluctance. Then he shrugged, took a sip of his wine, and looked directly at me.

"We all started out doing low-level stuff. We did simple tasks: report troop locations, material movements—you know, number of tanks and armored vehicles heading such and such direction, number of military officers staying in one town or city for how long, even stuff about crop yields and manufacturing quotas they considered important.

"But they gave higher clearance, higher pay, to those who would take greater risks, do, uh, tougher, uh, more sophisticated things."

"'Higher clearance'?"

"More authority. More access to sensitive material and information. More leeway in making on-the-spot decisions."

"I'd probably like that." I couldn't believe I'd said that. It just came out.

"I wouldn't be surprised."

Fr. Marshall leaned back and grinned. I was startled, my hands suddenly awkward, groping for another Pall Mall. Why did he say that? I tried to ignore the new feelings welling up within me and pushed the conversation.

"Does 'higher clearance' get into the James Bond stuff, you know, the 007 license to kill?"

"That part's not like in the books or the movies. Yes, they do have trained marksmen and a few who specialize in aggressive sabotage. But they're mostly ex-military specialists. The agency's more likely to hire out that kind of stuff, you know, to do the assassinations and terrorist stuff.

"They were up front about asking me to consider doing some of that higher level stuff in China, but I couldn't get myself to do it. Don't get me wrong. Those higher level guys did a good job in China."

"You didn't?"

"Oh, yes. But I wasn't there as long as they were. They were especially effective keeping the nuclear capability out of there for the longest time. They also had a lot to do with preventing the Korean business from becoming a total disaster."

Sitting across from me was a guy who had been there–literally. He was involved in all the action that had permeated my pre-teen imagination on Detroit's east side, images of machine gunning 'gooks'–my brother-in-law had actually done some of that stuff but would never talk about it–or of being like Gregory Peck in *Pork Chop Hill*. I began to feel something more than excitement, but I couldn't quite get at what it was exactly–a stirring of some kind, like colors and shapes and sounds I knew existed but hadn't yet experienced. It was almost like that feeling I had in lacrosse when I sensed a defenseman switching off his assignment and lining up my blind side, hoping to jolt me away from the goalie. It's something you can feel, but you don't *see*.

His persistent voice interrupted my thoughts.

"So what do you see yourself doing after graduation?"

"I've got a summer job lined up at Wolverine Tube in Detroit. After that I'm not sure. I already turned down a fellowship in English Lit at the University of Kansas."

"Why?"

"Uh, two reasons, I guess. One selfish, the other personal. I love literature, but I'm not sure I want to get into that really deep lit crit shit–pardon my French–and I'm so sick of school and studying I just can't imagine doing more of it right now. Besides, I should be helping out at home, you know, financially. I'm from a big family, and it wouldn't be fair to go running off to Kansas to get a master's or PhD and not help them out a little."

"Are you homesick or do they really need you? I mean, could they survive without that help?"

"I'm not sure why you're asking me that."

"I don't want to be presumptuous, but if you want to help your family and your country, there is a way, you know, I could put in a good word for you …"

"You mean …"

"Hey, you're an ideal candidate. They need people like you, people who have high ideals, high morals, willing to sacrifice, who are aggressive but not too fanatical, stuff like that."

"How can you say that? You really don't know me. I'm nowhere near smart enough to work for them nor am I that tough. How do you mean 'aggressive but not too fanatical'?"

"I know more about you than you think."

A strange, weird mixture of fear and anticipation invaded my senses, something like before a big game only more so. How many surprises did this guy have in him, anyway? He looked so ascetic, so priestly, but those eyes of his transcended that look; there was something impenetrable about him. I felt as though he could look into my very soul, that he could read my mind. But there was nothing reciprocal. I couldn't see into *him*. Not really. It made me uneasy. But I also felt something new and exciting.

Fr. Marshall pushed his chair back.

"Well, this was a great dinner and a very nice conversation, but I must get going. Let me drop you off at your place. It's right on the way to where I'm headed."

"Thanks. I really appreciate it. And this was more than a nice conversation—it's one of the most interesting conversations I've ever had in my life, believe me!"

Fr. Marshall's face lit up with a grin.

"My pleasure."

* * *

The letter from Sacred Heart Seminary arrived Monday.

Dear Sean,
Greetings from SHS and your old English teacher. Thought you'd like to know some government types stopped by this afternoon after classes and asked questions about you—said you were applying for a government job that was 'medium security'—whatever that means!
I told them the truth—be calm, now—it was all compliments! But something about the two guys made me a bit uneasy, and I thought I should let you know.
I called your parents to get your address, but I didn't tell them anything. They say you're graduating in June. I'm glad to hear that, but if you're in any difficulty, let me know, and I'll do what I can to help.

God Bless,
Fr. Frank (Fracassa)

That night, I brought the letter with me to class to show Fr. Marshall, but he wasn't there. After class, I hustled back to my room and looked up the phone number of St. Michael's Seminary. I didn't think anyone would answer that late in the evening, but a seminary student was manning the phones. He was very pleasant when I apologized about the late hour, explaining that they kept the lines open until at least midnight in case one of the priests was called out on an emergency at the hospital. When I asked if I could speak with Fr. Marshall, he sounded puzzled. "You mean Fr. Mitchell? M-I-T-C-H-E-L-L?"

"No, Marshall. M-A-R-S-H-A-L-L. He teaches English Literature there and is taking grad classes at St. Catherine's."

"I'm sorry, sir. I've been a seminarian here for over four years. Believe me: no Fr. Marshall teaches here, and no one on staff is presently taking any classes at St. Catherine College. Sounds like someone may be handing you a line. Know what I mean?"

"Yes. I know what you mean. Thanks."

"Sorry I couldn't be of more help."

I hung up the phone and smiled. I took a quick peek out my second story apartment window and looked around at all the shadows out there in the night, checking to see if anyone were "casing the joint." I didn't see anyone or anything. I began to wonder when the next contact would come.

Chapter 5

Carolyn Carrington

My Name Is ...

In English my name means melody and joy.
It is like the number seven. It means music.
It means a song.
It means a bright and happy tune.

It was my grandmother's middle name.
I was named after a great lady.
She was an exuberant, positive thinking
         and
      a talking woman, too;

She was born like me in the month of January.
She liked to laugh and smile a lot!
She was just like that!
She brought joy to other people.
         Carolyn
    I have inherited her name.

At school sometimes they confuse my name with
         Caroline.
This pronunciation sounds very formal–like
      Queen Caroline or Princess Caroline.

If I could baptize myself under a new name, the real me
                nobody sees,
    I think I'd still be
            Carolyn!

A First Day in the Life of a Kindergartner

The halls are clean. There are at least two layers of newly applied wax on the tile floors. These had been filled with scuffs and spills of all kinds last June. The hallways have been quiet for at least two months. The outer world was absent from this place!

The bell rings faintly. Someone asks, "Was that the bell?" Babbling voices echo throughout the hall: the quiet chatter of the tiny voices of children. Footsteps are heard, both of anxious children and nervous parents. A new school year is about to begin. New children are coming! New children are coming!

Some children are entering the school after a year in Pre-School or a year in Head Start to begin another year of experiences. A new group of five year olds will walk hurriedly down the hall and enter into the classroom. They will be apprehensive about how their first time away from mother's loving care will unfold. The first day in the life of a kindergartener is about to begin.

As the children finally enter their classroom and take a quick peripheral look around at the toys and books, they may think, "I can play all day." But kindergarten is more than play.

The children are not aware of the fact they will practice and learn to follow the leader as they walk in a straight line. They are not aware of the fact that they must master the art of walking behind their classmates so as not to step on anyone's heels or toes. Each kindergarten student will have to keep his hands and feet to himself or herself; or maybe even folded during specific times of the day! They will practice raising their hand for permission to share thoughts and ideas and, sometimes, special events in their life.

They will play with interlocking wooden multicolored blocks, both large and small. They will move puzzle pieces around on a wooden board to fit into specially carved-out spaces. Moving magnetic letters into alphabetical order and spelling their name correctly will be an exciting venture during "centers time" as they master alphabet recognition.

The new students will learn that red is the color of an apple, a crayon, a new pencil for today's handwriting lesson, the cover of our story time book, the bulletin board paper, and Mary's red dress. They will learn that scissors and paste are used after a mantra of do's and don'ts is completed. Only one student at a time will demonstrate this skill to the class. One student will use a pair of scissors at a time following a straight vertical line to the edge of the paper. The paste must be used carefully and cautiously. The children will learn they will not bluff the substitute teacher into letting everyone use scissors at the same time and walk around the room with scissors in hand after the completion of a cut and paste project.

These kindergarteners will use paint as they learn the colors red, yellow, blue, green, orange, purple, white, and black. They will mentally paint beautiful pictures. Early sightings of scribbles and lines will welcome the start of beginning writing experiences. They will dream, think, and imagine new, purposeful beginnings each day.

Most kindergarteners quickly realize they cannot play with the puzzles, bounce the balls, color with crayons, paint neatly, jump rope, take quiet naps, use the lavatory, play with blocks, complete art projects, and ask questions without first learning about the "how" and "why" of caring, sharing, and listening.

Lessons for life are taught early!

An Alphabet Poem to a New Kindergartner from a First Grade Student

Always be courageous.
Don't ever forget: great handwriting is just keen.
Love making number orders.
Play, question, read, study.
Think uniquely.
Venture with excitement.
Yield!
Zeal!

Chapter 6

Mary Cox

Shattered

Where was the booster seat? She stood in the middle of the kitchen with her hands on her hips. She supposed that one of the children had taken it upstairs or outside to play with. She shook her head and went back to setting the table.

There was a smell. She was very fastidious in her housekeeping, and smells always annoyed her. She looked under the kitchen sink and gathered the garbage bag. She knew she had reminded Tom to take the garbage out this morning before he went to work. She carried the bag to the back door. She would take it out herself in a few minutes. When she returned, she put the dishes on the table.

Where was her spoon?

She sat down at the table. She was tired today. She moved a fork and spoon to different sides of a dish. She watched her reflection in the face of the plate and automatically drew her finger around its edge. The uneven surface distorted her face. Her nose seemed broader; her eyes were heavily lidded. The plate-mirror bleached out her skin and hair. This is what she would look like when she got old. She ran her hand through her hair. It felt brittle. She needed to have it conditioned. With three young children, she just wasn't able to get any time for herself.

She shook herself. How long had she been sitting here? She needed to move on. She collected a plate and put it in the sink, then took a spoon and stirred a pot. The kitchen was hot. She wiped her face.

Standing in front of the sink, she looked out the window. For a while she was lost in thought, picturing the children running after each other, rolling in the grass, splashing in the little plastic swimming pool that stayed up all summer, leaving a permanent circle in the grass. She turned her eyes to that spot and suffered a moment of confusion.

The yard looked strange to her. Something was different.

She needed to get out there and trim the hedges. They were encroaching on the yard from all sides. The yard looked smaller, confined. Suddenly, tears sprang to her eyes. She'd been this way all day, weepy and "antsy" as her mother would say. She watched a cat pick its way through the tall grass in the yard and smiled.

Julia loved cats. She turned to call to her daughter to come and see the kitty. She was suddenly struck by the silence in the house. This much quiet was never a good sign with children. She listened intently for the sound of stifled giggles or talking or footsteps over her head. Nothing.

She headed down the hall to go upstairs. At the turn in the hallway, she suddenly felt panicked. Her heart beat heavily; she leaned against the wall, her breath coming in short pants. She wanted to sink to the floor and hide her face from the strange place she found herself in. She felt disoriented, lost. She closed her eyes against the strangeness she saw, and dragging her hand along the wall she felt her way back to the kitchen. She fell into a chair.

What was wrong with her? What was happening? She took a deep breath, slowly calming down. When her heart had slowed and her breathing returned to normal, she opened her eyes. For a moment her heart began to speed up, and then gradually, as she looked at her familiar curtains and her grandmother's frying pan on the stove, she calmed and felt better.

She rested her head on her hands. What was this? Why was she having these attacks? She'd read about women with post-partum depression, but her youngest, Tommy, was six months. Wasn't that too long?

It was the ringing that broke into her thoughts. She looked around. The phone? Where was it? There was urgency in the sound that agitated her. She looked frantically. Then the pounding started on the door. Not a friendly knocking, but a dangerous banging. Someone was yelling. And the ringing! She covered her ears. There was so much noise.

Glass shattered. Now she could hear a man's voice over the incessant ringing. Her heart beat faster. Someone was breaking into the house! The phone, if she answered the phone she could tell whoever was there to call for help.

She lifted herself, leaning on the table. The plates were too close to the edge. Her movement caused them to crash to the floor. She looked down at the shattered pottery around her feet. For a moment she couldn't understand what had happened, and then the back door swung violently open and banged against the wall. She turned and fled the kitchen.

She felt lost in her own house. Her sight was dimming. She looked down the hall through a haze. The hall seemed to go in strange directions. It was like a nightmare in which she was pursued by an unseen attacker. She had to control her panic.

"Find the phone, get help," she told herself. "Find the children; get them out of the house!" In her panic, walls seemed to close in; rugs caught at her feet. She tripped and fell heavily against the wall. She turned to look behind her. A man was approaching down the hall.

"No!" she screamed. "Children, run! Get out of the house! Hurry!"

As he reached for her, she kicked out, flailing her arms and scratching at his face, but he overpowered her and wrapped his arms around her, pinning her to his side. She gasped; she couldn't breathe. Panic rose up in her and she felt herself slipping into unconsciousness.

* * *

Tom Martin sat in a kitchen chair amid broken dishes. The smoke alarm was now silent, but a haze still hung near the ceiling. The smell of burnt metal filled the kitchen, and two pans had melted together to form a strange abstract sculpture on the stove burners. Food was spread across the counter in various stages of preparation. A bowl of flour and water sat congealing. It would soon be impossible to separate the paste from the bowl. Peeled potatoes lay in the sink turning brown. A large dollop of grease melted on the floor in front of the stove, making a dangerous slippery spot. The curtains, slightly singed from the flames, billowed softly into the room. The window, opened to let out the smoke, also relieved the smell of rotting garbage.

Tom knew that if he turned his head, he would be able to look down the hall and see the torn gauze packages, tubing, and rubber gloves the EMS workers had left behind after they removed his 83 year old mother to the hospital. If he lived to be 100, he would never forget the terrified look on her face as she ran from him down the hall. He had tried to stop her, to tell her who he was, but she had not recognized him at all.

He lifted himself heavily from the chair. He needed to get to the hospital. His sisters would be there by now, and there would be lots of hard decisions to make. A tear escaped and ran down his cheek. He was overcome with a great sense of loss and guilt.

Chapter 7

Ahna Felix-Brown

Lifetime

July 8 Marks

the day

2 became 1

2 minds–1 thought

2 souls–1 life

2 hearts–1 beat

2 bodies–1 complete entity

1 lifetime spent–

2gether

4ever.

Dream Fulfilled

Girls' night out
is now Girl's night in.
Work-related stress
no longer important.
December 6, 2001, my world forever changed.
Now
Warm tender hugs soothe–
Bouquets of gentle caresses calm–
I
never knew a love like this.
Joy!
Rapture!
Jubilee!
–I can't wait for you to whisper,
"Mommy."

A Thoughtful Alphabet Poem
(For Ariana–silver, holy one, breath of air.)

Angelic being: child.
Distinctive, Extraordinary, Flawless.
God's handiwork.
Illuminating jewel.
Kaleidoscopic landscape; Miracle
Necessitates osculation.
Play quells remorse.
Silver turns unsatisfaction valueless.
Welcome exalted youth!
Zephyrus.

A to Z

Ariana
My
Beautiful child
Delivered especially for
Guidance

Humility
Instruction

She
Kindles love
Maternal nurturing
Over-protection

She
Redeems spirit
Teaches uplifting virtues
a-
wakens excitement; youthfulness
Zoe

Beautiful Reflection
(For Ariana & Betty)

Almond shaped eyes
    Dipped in chocolate
    No wonder why
    I'm so mesmerized.

Chubby cheeks
    With permanent blush
    No wonder why
    I must always touch.

Honey sweet voice
    So warm and full of laughter
    No wonder why
    I live to hear you call "MOMMY!"

Sun-kissed skin
    Caressed by its warmth
    No wonder why
    I call you café mocha and caramel delight.

You beguile me
>   Delight me
>   Holy one.

Your hugs, your smile, your love
>   Invite me
>   Silver one.

You fulfill my dreams
>   Airy one.

I was Granny's and now
You are my beautiful reflection.

Reflection Pt. 2

Mommy, "You're a superhero!"
I smile and melt
For in my daughter's eyes
I am invincible

Mommy, "I love you!"
I smile and melt
For in my daughter's eyes
I am treasured

Mommy, "You rock!"
I laugh out loud and shake my head
For in my daughter's eyes
I am everything

Mommy, "You're awesome!"
I laugh out loud and shake my head
For in my daughter's eyes
I am perfect

What she doesn't know
Is that she was sent to rescue me
In her eyes,
I am everything I want to be

What she doesn't know
Is that she creates peace
In her eyes,
I find reasons to believe

What she doesn't know
Is that in her eyes
I see the future; a reflection
Of who I'll be
Everything that she has made me

Untitled

In my mother's eyes
I am the perfect woman
Strong, wise, fearless
Ready to take on the world
Isn't it plain to see?
She is all I ever wanted to be

In my mother's eyes
I am powerful
I turn darkness to light
Bringing knowledge to the innocent
Doesn't she see?
She is all of that to me

In my mother's eyes
I can see the future
A reflection of who I'll be
I already know
I'm all she intended me to be

You Loved Me First

You loved me first
sight unseen.
I loved you back
not knowing me.

After so many tries
that met with failure.
God saw fit
to join Us together.

Pillows and prayers
went hand in hand.
We made it through
it was His master plan.

December Nineteenth
smiles all around.
I was handed to you
tightly bound.

Little Brown baby
in a red stocking.
You took me home
to give more loving.

I'm so grateful
for your love and care.
Always know that
I am there.

I forget to call
and even write.
I promise you're in
my heart every day and night.

I love you so much
mere words will never convey.
I love you so much
more than I can say.

You loved me first
now I'm all grown up.
I love you back
for you fill me up.

You're my hero, my light
my very first love.
I know you were sent
from heaven above.

You loved me first
it's grown deeper by the year.
I'll love you forever more
Mommy dear.

Daddy's Girl

I love my daddy that's
no lie.
I've always been the apple
of his eye.

I love my daddy;
he was the first—the first
to state
my true worth.

O, how I love my daddy.
I've truly been blessed
to know his love's
sweet caress.

He's gentle and kind
and so full of wit.
He and I are
a perfect fit.

O, how I love my daddy.
I don't tell him enough.
He's an angel that watched
me through the rough stuff.

I love my daddy.
to make sure that he knows

I sat down and wrote
this poem.

Love,
Your Chocolate Chip

Did You Know?

Did you know?
You are my everything
From believer of my dreams
To bringer of ice cream

Did you know?
You are my everything
From protector of scary monsters
To perfect provider

Did you know?
You are my everything
Thanks for time spent
And cookies sent

Did you know?
There could never be
A daughter who loved
Her father more than me

What's in a Name?

A name so short, yet so complex; a name that has caused me grief, but brought adoration; a name that makes certain I am original and like no other–distinguished. It has a beautiful sound as it rolls off the tongue, almost like a musical note or a sigh of relief; Ahna. A-H-N-A. It simply means grace and truth. What mother wouldn't wish this for her only daughter?

My mother thought long and deeply about my destiny, for my mother descends from French Creole ancestry and believes that names should create a person's fate, not be a cross to bear. Named after my grandmother and an aunt, I became Ahna. Mommy changed the spelling so that Americans would pronounce it as it should be; the French or Spanish way. It didn't work! Everyone still pronounces it incorrectly, and worse yet, they are certain that I'm spelling it wrong. Even family members couldn't get it quite right. Mommy would often get frustrated and say, "How can I expect the world to get it, when family can't?"

I often changed to adapt to this imperfect world, and in doing so, I changed, gained, or lost a piece of myself, each time. In elementary school, I started printing in capital letters. [A practice I still continue to this day.] My teachers thought that I was simply making the stem on my "h" too long, so to help them understand their mistake, I reasoned, "A capital H certainly looks nothing like a capital N right?"

Wrong! They were too concerned with the forest to see the trees. In other words, they felt that my penmanship would suffer if I didn't practice upper and lower case letters. Forget about my self-esteem because they didn't care enough to get my name right. By the time they really comprehended, it was close to the end of the school term, and the start of each new year guaranteed that my trauma would start afresh with a brand new teacher. This cycle played itself out over and over and over again like a broken record on a turntable.

After much drama, in college I became "A. Michelle." At this point in life, the stakes became much too high. One year I visited the university hospital with an extremely sore throat. I was examined and diagnosed with strep throat. Because of my pain and probably the fever, I simply gave my name.

Three days later, I thought my ear would burst. Yes, I know that I had not finished my prescription, but I was certain my ear shouldn't feel that way. I returned to the hospital stating, "I was seen here three days ago by a doctor. My ear is now in a lot of pain. I believe my infection has spread."

The nurse sat at her computer and typed; looked at me intently, typed some more and looked at me again.

"Are you sure you were seen here?"

"Yes." I impatiently replied.

More nurses came and eventually a doctor; they seemed puzzled. Again, I was asked if I had my time frame right because I simply did not exist in the computer. They had gone back two to three weeks, and my name just wasn't in the system. Now, my mother would have truly been ashamed, for I shouted indignantly, "I'm not some crack addict who is coming off of a high and can't remember what they've done or where they've been! I was seen in this damn hospital three days ago, and I want someone to help me immediately!"

Now I'm sure that I looked the part of an addict, and with my sudden outburst, I'm certain they weren't so sure that I wasn't one. It was then that I had an epiphany. I quietly asked, "Is my name spelled correctly?"

A bright light suddenly filled the room as angels came down singing, "Hallelujah, Hallelujah!" One of those days (I didn't care to find out which), someone had spelled my name wrong; the other correctly. Even though I was one person physically, they had me on record as two completely distinct individuals and on two separate charts.

My name has even caused me to miss a plane. Mommy forgot to make certain it was spelled correctly. Yeah, right. Instead of listening, the reservation representative just decided, like the rest of the world, that she knew how to spell my name better than my mother did. I showed up at the airport, handed over my ID and was promptly told that I, Ahna, had no reservation.

"What?! My mother reserved this ticket a month ago."

"Well, she didn't spell your name correctly."

The idea of my own mother's not spelling her only daughter's name correctly was completely ludicrous. I mean, the audacity to make such a statement. I started to ask the woman, "When did my mother make the mistake? At my birth or when she made the reservation for me?"

To add insult to injury, because my mother had placed the reservation on her credit card, I couldn't change it. I couldn't change my own name! As luck would have it, Mommy wasn't home when I called.

I sat, watched people check-in, board the plane, and fumed as it backed away from the gate and subsequently flew away. I was incensed. I'd had enough. People couldn't possibly get A. Michelle wrong. That's it; that's the ticket. I'll become A. Michelle.

Obviously, people aren't smart enough to see their mistakes, so I'll adapt. But there are so many Michelles in the world. How would people know which one was me? Had I lost myself? Was I still an original? Was I still me? An even better question was, why did I have to adapt?

What the world must see is that a name truly distinguishes and creates personality. It is a person's most prized possession, for it survives even death. A name should not be played with and thrown around carelessly. It is an insult to the person because that person understands you just couldn't even take the time to listen.

My name is uniquely me. It is different and unlike any other. And that's me; the left-handed woman who often marches to a very different beat. The feminist who loves hip-hop music, rock 'n' roll, and the blues equally; I'm an idealist and optimist who sees many situations through rose-colored glasses. The high maintenance girly-girl who reveres football, basketball, and even boxing; I am straightforward, generous, and in love with love. I'm positively certain there is a Cornucopia of Plenty, and a Fountain of Youth. I just haven't found it. Don't get me wrong. I'm no Pollyanna. The world is certainly not perfect. Neither am I, but I am the person who distinctly knows who her friends are because they know how to pronounce my name. I am even the person who found love because the first time my husband approached me he pronounced it correctly.

I no longer care if the world gets it right. For you see, I'm now distinctly me: an original, like no other.

I'm glad to be me because what you see is what my mother intended me to be: graceful, truthful, and so much more. So Ahna is what I choose to be.

Destiny Designation

"Why are you so quiet this evening?" he asks as we sit in the parking lot of Blockbuster in early spring. My stepson is visiting for Spring Break and has decided that our cable stations are "whack," and our video collection even worse. I respond by saying something so abstract that my husband looks at me with complete bewilderment.

"OK. What's wrong?"

"Nothing."

"That's not true. You're not yourself. You're not talking and you're starting to remind me of a space cadet."

I continue to look off into space. His patented response flows from his lips: "I've known you long enough to know when something's bothering you."

"Just thinking. That's all."

"Come on now. How long have we been married?"

"Long enough to make a baby," I quietly mention.

It's just then that Mark Jr. hops back in the car, perfectly ecstatic over his video finds. My husband starts the car, pulls out of the space, and heads out of the parking lot toward home. After driving half way home, my response finally hits him.

"Long enough to ... Did you mean something by that statement?"

"Did you just get that?"

"You know who you married. You gotta tell it to me straight."

"True enough, but that was slow even for you."

We were expecting a baby; my first, his second. I knew life would never be quite the same. The journey with my daughter began that night, but it wouldn't take long to get more complicated.

I believe, as my mother did, that naming a child is of the utmost importance because it is more than just some word attached to a body. One's reputation centers around one's name.

A name is a label that a person carries for life. Consequently, it is a person's most valuable possession, for it is the only thing that survives the death. A name has the power to shape personality, influence success, and others' perceptions.

As a result, choosing a name for my child was my first and most important responsibility as a parent. My daughter would have name for a lifetime, so I had to choose one she'd be proud to have. One people wouldn't whisper about or shake their heads in disbelief when they hear it.

Words couldn't describe my elation, knowing I was expecting my first child. For the first three months my husband and I bantered back and forth about the baby's sex. He strongly felt that it would be a boy, so there was no need to figure out a girl's name. He used some strange old wives' tale that I'd never even heard of.

"Besides," he states sarcastically, "God wouldn't give me two of you."

At this, I gently remind him that it's extremely difficult to sleep with a pillow over his head. I press on, ignoring him and continuing to think of names. Going on his intuition, we concentrate on boy's names.

"Since you're so certain it's a boy, what will be his name?"

"Mark III."

"You already have a Mark Jr., and correct me if I'm wrong, you're not related to George Foreman." For one complete month we go back and forth, back and forth.

"No. No. Hell no!" I call out.

"No. No. Are you nuts?" he tells me.

Finally one day it just came. "What about Miles Xavier Wingfield?" Ooh! That sounds nice. It's strong and sounds masculine; Miles means "soldier" while Xavier means "bright." That's a wonderful prophecy for a man-child.

We settled on that, both of us quite happy, but then I said, "Well, what if we have a girl?"

"A girl? You're not having a girl."

"OK, Mr. Smarty pants. We'll just see about that when we go have the ultrasound."

Wouldn't you know it? God likes to play practical jokes. The ultrasound confirmed that we were having a girl, a girl–a sweet little girl. What do I want her be?

"What about Jasmine?"

"No."

"Ashley?"

"Too many."

"A unisex name might be good, like Taylor, Sidney, or even Kennedy."

"No, no and no."

"What about Aaliyah? That's really a great name. It's beautiful, has a musical quality, and means 'to ascend, exalted.'" He nods and says that's the name of that singer.

"Do we want to name her after a singer?"

"Why not? We were going to name the boy after a musician."

"You got a point. I like it."

"I'll think about a good middle name."

Months pass. I have nothing concrete yet. As I doze on my couch in late August, I hear the newscaster say something that I must have heard wrong. It jolts me from drowsiness.

"Aaliyah Dana Houghton is dead."

She's too young to be dead. She was killed in a plane crash after a video shoot. The plane was too heavy. What is this madness? He must have some bad information. I switch channels, but sure enough. It is breaking news, just coming over the wire. Aaliyah is dead.

This changes everything. The outpouring of sorrow was intense, especially because I teach in the high school that Aaliyah graduated from. There were candlelight vigils, a growing memorial, people crying, and grief counselors. I knew I'd have to find a new name. Everyone would give newborn daughters her name, now that she's gone. I want my daughter to stand out, be distinguishable.

"What about naming her after our grandmothers?"

"Aria? Already got one on my side; besides you'd be upset because the family doesn't pronounce it the way you do."

"Oh. This girl is going to come into the world without a name. My grandmother's name is my name, just spelled Anna. I'm like my mother. I want it pronounced as it should be, so that's not the way to go."

What about a combination of names? That would be different. Aria means "a song," "a melody for a single voice," or "a breath of air." I think that's so pretty. Anna, whichever way you spell it, means "grace, truth." That's a great destiny. I got worried though. What if this was some offensive name when joined? I got lucky–it wasn't.

When I searched for the name, I got more than what I'd bargained for. Ariana is a name that originates from French and Greek meaning "holy one, exalted." It is also Hebrew, meaning "silver," which is a precious metal mentioned in the Bible. Her middle name became my grandmother's nickname, Zoe. It is also of Greek origin, meaning "life."

That's a name a girl can be proud of, no matter how it's broken down. That's a designation a girl can grow into; she can transcend the mundane of the everyday and become a remarkable woman.

She is my little "holy one," most precious in my sight.

Chapter 8

Catherine Haar

Poems for Libby, Who's One Year Old

    Pickle
You put it in your mouth
And shiver
Down to your toes.
Then you smile, grab
The pickle, and put it
Back in your mouth.

    Crackle
Dry leaves, left over on the lawn.
You pick them up
And pull.
They rip, they crackle
You giggle in glee
And rip leaf after leaf.

    Treasure
Outside, you search
For treasure on the lawn.
A wood chip, a rock,
One for each hand.
You carry them with you
As you walk.

Then, when you go inside
You place them down
Ever so carefully
Back where they live.

      Talking
A day before your birthday
You walk to the front door
Where your dad has left for work.
You look, you wave your hand,
And you say, "Da-de, Da-de."
Then you do it again
At the window.
Quite satisfied with yourself
You return to play.

      Your Day
All day you're cheerful and busy.
Play, eat, nap.
Eat, nap, play.
You gather your doll
And your book and
Trundle into your
Small chair.
You push the buttons
To make music play.
Then Ty the dog gets all excited
And so do you.
Through the door comes
Mom, and you say
"Hi" and wave and smile
And meet her at the door.

On the Sudden Death of a Friend

You can't guard against death.
It's the secret seed
At life's core. It's
Out the back door.

It's at lunch
In the succulent bunch
Of grapes you eat.
It's down the cellar steps,
Up the attic, in the drawer.

If you guard against death
The seed sleeps as before.
(It wakes when it will.)
But the doing-so bleeds into the day
Soaks the night down to the sheets
Pulses into everything
Books, gardening, cooking, working, thinking
And you can't find your life anymore.

Thoreau Was Right: An ABC Poem

Anomalous boxes.
Closets, dreadfully engorged.
Files: grotesque, horrible.
Information, junk, kitsch,
Languishing, moldering, nagging.
Overwhelming piles.
Queerly residing, stifling, thwarting,
Undercutting valuable work.
Exit yesterday's zone!

The Five-Paragraph Theme: A Comment

For poems
Anything goes.
So why are we so
Strict with prose?

Poets might
Elect free verse.
But essayists boxed
In the hearse
Of stipulated forms

Of Scottish rhetoricians
Are stuck for words
And thoughts are apparitions.
And left to dry
Are structured lines, bland wordings, and transitions.

Forms have uses, no dispute.
I wouldn't give them all the boot.
This doggerel I wrote by rule
Using what I learned in school.
But no one form should reign supreme
Crowding others from the scene.
Ideas need to seek out form
With writers' choices as the norm.

Chapter 9

Kathy Hribar

Sundays with Grandma

The roast beef and mashed potatoes are resting comfortably in my stomach. The table is cleared, the leftovers put away, the dishwasher loaded. Now comes the time I've been waiting for all evening ... now comes my favorite time with Grandma. Is Grandma going to help me bake chocolate chip cookies? Crochet a potholder? No, not my grandmother. My grandma is going to let me in on a grown-up pastime most other ten year-olds don't get to experience ... *playing poker*. I feel like one of those kids whose parents take them to R-rated movies, except my parents don't do that, so I'll have to settle for poker.

"Poker," you're thinking. "Isn't that for the rough-and-tumble men of the family, carefully studying both cards and opponents while they puff on Cuban cigars?" [Just so you know, no one in my family actually smokes cigars.] Well, my grandmother grew up with five brothers, so she learned a thing or two about poker, if not cigars. And she learned a thing or two about holding her own with the men. "She just learned to talk louder than them," my dad would say.

Yes, my grandmother's strong, confident voice fills up her entire house, which isn't really that big. It's a two-bedroom bungalow in East Detroit, only a few miles from my house. Almost every Sunday we go over there, and I wait for her to shout my favorite words: "Go find the pennies! It's time to play!"

I set out in search of the change purse, a blue and green beaded sack filled with pennies, opened only on special poker-playing occasions. It's sometimes hard to find the change purse in Grandma's house. She has an awful lot of stuff packed into a very small space. I start searching in the living room, on top of the stereo. I peek under stacks of *National Enquirer* magazines, and notebooks filled with daily gas meter readings. "Always read the gas meter yourself," Grandma tells me. "You can't trust the gas company." Or the phone company, I've come to learn. Or the bank.

"I think the pennies are on the table at the top of the stairs," Grandma calls out to me. Uh-oh. This means trouble. The stairs are like those obstacle courses we sometimes run in gym class. I step over the extra pairs of house slippers, the bottles of Absopure water, the pile of telephone books, and the broken toaster. I finally locate the change purse and head back downstairs.

Grandma is sitting at the kitchen table. She's wearing her usual polyester blouse, pulled tightly across her large frame. It's purple, of course (her favorite color), accented with a few spots of gravy. But who cares? Her hair is a beautiful shade of champagne blonde. I always thought the color was natural until I saw the L'Oreal box in her bathroom, shade 8 1/2 A. "Never let anyone know your true age," she always tells me. I'm sure I'll appreciate this advice when I'm older, though I'm not too concerned at ten years of age.

My older sisters, Mary Beth and Michelle, are also sitting at the table. My mom has taken my little sister, Carrie, out in the backyard to play. Carrie's a little young yet for poker. Dad and Grandpa are sitting close by in the living room, watching TV. They don't play cards with us. They love Grandma, but after so many years with her, they just need a little space. I guess I can understand.

Grandma opens a box of worn-out Bicycle cards and starts shuffling. I count out the pennies, twenty per person. Somehow those twenty cents feel like a small fortune.

"OK, it's baseball first," Grandma announces. "Seven-card stud, threes and nines are wild."

"Grandma, why is it threes and nines?" I ask.

"Three outs, nine innings," Dad calls from the living room. He can't resist responding to a sports-related question.

"I thought you weren't playing," Grandma retorts. "It's just me and the girls."

She smiles as she deals out two cards in the hole, and one card face up. I study my cards intently, trying to decide how much I should bet.

"Kathy, you're too serious," Grandma tells me. "You need to smile." Grandma's always telling me that. When I was eight years old Grandma gave me a smile can. It was a homemade bank that she put a dime into every time she caught me smiling. I didn't really like it, but Grandma thought it was a good idea, so I went along with it.

We go around the table, each one of us taking our turn betting. Grandma continues dealing one card at a time. Halfway through the hand, Grandma and Mary Beth fold. Now it's just Michelle and me, anxiously waiting for our last card in the hole.

"Here it comes, down and dirty," Grandma announces in her animated voice. To my disappointment, Michelle's full house beats my two pair, so she rakes in the huge pot.

"Grandma, you better watch out for Michelle. She's going to join the Bilderbergers," I joke. The Bilderbergers are these really rich people who are taking over the world, though nobody knows about them. Except Grandma, of course.

"Go ahead and laugh," she says. "You'll see. One day they will form one world government and one World Bank. They killed JFK, you know." I don't really know what all this means. I just know I like to get Grandma going.

"OK, my turn to deal," Michelle says. "Dime store. Fives and tens are wild." She starts passing out cards.

"Hey, speaking of dime store, I met this cashier at Fairway last week," Grandma tells me. "She told me about this great recipe of hers for chicken soup."

"How did you start talking about chicken soup?" I ask.

"It's because I'm interested in people's lives," she says, slightly annoyed. "I don't know what's wrong with the rest of you. You never ask any questions."

I think it's kind of embarrassing how Grandma stops to talk to everyone she meets. But if I get some good chicken soup out of it, then it's OK.

We go around the table and place our bets. I've got two nines in the hole, so I'm feeling pretty lucky, though I try to hide my excitement. Luckily the attention is diverted from me when Mary Beth starts to cough.

"Mary Beth, you still have that cough? Have you gone to the doctor yet?" Grandma quizzes her. Grandma is always concerned about our health. If there's the slightest breeze outside, she makes us put on a babushka. That's the word Polish grandmothers use for a scarf, except we're not Polish. If we give the slightest complaint of a sore throat, Grandma paints our tonsils with Mercurochrome.

"I'm fine, Grandma," Mary Beth replies.

"You know what I keep telling all of you ... B12 shots, that's the key to good health. I've got to go to Dr. Mishra next week and get my shot. While I'm there, I'm going to make him give me another neck X-ray. My neck hasn't been right since I took that fall last month ..."

"Hey Grandma, it's your turn to bet," I tell her. Early on, I learned that diversion is a useful tactic.

"All right, Kathy," Grandma chirps happily. "I'll see your two pennies, and I'll raise you five."

"WHAT? Five? I can't afford that!" I complain.

"Hey, what's all the noise in there?" Dad calls from the living room.

"It's Grandma. She's trying to clean me out," I lament.

"You can always come in here and watch baseball with us," Dad says, kidding, knowing I won't leave the table.

"There you go, trying to turn her into a sports nut, just like you and your father," Grandma replies. "She's staying in here with me. Kathy's a Libra, and Libra belongs with Gemini." Gemini is Grandma's sign.

I don't put much stock in astrology, but somehow when Grandma talks about it, I believe it. I like the idea that it was written in the stars for us to be together. I win the hand with four kings, so it's my turn to deal.

"Low hole card," I announce.

"You know I hate that game!" Grandma says. "Just when you think your hand is all set, you get that last card and it screws up everything."

"I know you hate it," I reply with a smug grin. "That's why I always choose it."

As we go around the table for another hand, I sit back quietly and take in the conversation. It jumps around like a Super Mario video game. I hear about Aunt Ruthie's new dog, the price of meat at A&P, and the fairy-tale wedding of Charles and Diana. I learn that FDR was the greatest President we ever had, and that Social Security saved our country from financial disaster. I want the poker game to keep going. I want to hear the conversation keep swirling around me, but Dad announces that it's time to go.

"Remember, Mom, we're leaving on vacation next week," Dad says.

"I know," she replies sadly. "I have my candle ready, so I can keep it lit while you're gone." Grandma always lights a candle and puts it right in front of our family picture whenever we go away. She prays for us and worries about us … a lot. I remember Dad telling me about this one time when he and Mom went camping with Uncle Dave and Aunt Dawn. A state trooper knocked on the door of their trailer at 5:00 a.m., saying that Grandma had had a premonition of a gas leak, and begged him to check on them.

"Don't worry, Grandma, we'll be fine," I assure her.

"Oh, my Kathy," she sighs, "what would I ever do without you?"

"You'll never have to find out," I answer, as she folds her arms around me in a tight embrace.

Grandma's hugs are softer than any pillow I've ever felt. I can smell her unique scent: Estée Lauder perfume mixed with bacon grease from cooking. I can hear the rhythm of her heartbeat, the heart that she says sometimes loves too much, but I wouldn't have it any other way.

    I gather up the pennies and put them back in the change purse. I notice that a few beads have fallen off the purse over the years, but it's still beautiful. And as I feel the weight of those pennies in my hand, I know that I am rich beyond my wildest dreams.

Grandma Rose and Her Apple Tree: A Poem for Two Voices

I never thought I was beautiful.
Large nose, size ten feet
Passed over as just ordinary.
But my family made me beautiful.
Bob, gliding me across the dance floor
Kathy, resting against my shoulder
While I cradled her,
Singing.

                                          I never thought I was special.
                                          Rough bark, common fruit
                                          Noticed mostly by squirrels.
                                          But her family made me special.
                                          Rose, throwing picnics under my canopy
                                          Kathy, leaning against my trunk
                                          While I protected her,
                                          Shading.

I've never experienced such pain.
Slow-burning flames invade my limbs
Every movement is torture.
My family, aching to comfort me
My doctors, attempting to diagnose me
Finally, one discovers the answer—
Cancer,
Eating away my bones.

	I've never encountered such blight.
Dried-out branches lead to withered leaves
Even my fruit is sickly.
Her family, hoping to revive me
Her landscaper, trying to examine me
Finally, he pinpoints the problem—
Worms,
Consuming my wood.
I never expected to live this long.	*I never expected to live this long.*
Hip rebuilt, neck irradiated
My embrace has lost its strength.	
	Pests killed, limbs amputated
My shadow has shrunk in size.
I could give up on life,
say it's not worth the effort	*I could give up on life,*
say it's not worth the effort
But I am their source of hope	
	And I am their link to memories
So here I stand,	*So here I stand,*
Surviving.	*Surviving.*

Upon the Emptying of My Grandma's House

The world no longer let me love;
My hope and Treasure lies above.
-Anne Bradstreet, "Verses Upon the Burning of Our House"

 From a high school American Literature anthology the size of a telephone book, these lines from Anne Bradstreet are the only specific words that I can remember. Why did these words make such an impression on me? Why did they find permanent storage in my brain? Perhaps it's because, at the age of 15, I found the mindset of the poet quite astonishing.

Here was a woman who had lost her home, along with all her worldly possessions, and yet held onto her faith and optimism. I must not be a very religious person, I thought, despite my Catholic upbringing. My home—a blond brick ranch on Johnston Street—provided a haven of security and comfort. I couldn't imagine it suddenly disappearing from my life.

At the age of 33, I have taken this quotation out of the storage closets of memory. The lines again make me question my beliefs as I ponder the future of my grandmother's house. One year ago, just before her diagnosis of cancer, Grandma reluctantly acknowledged that she could no longer take care of herself in her own home. She left behind a white aluminum-sided bungalow on Toepfer Avenue, her haven for 63 years. She currently lives in a senior residence, bravely struggling to maintain optimism while the specter of cancer shadows her. Yet the house on Toepfer, minus her furniture, now at the senior residence, remains much as it did on the day that she left it.

Why hasn't the home been sold? I've asked myself that question many times. At first, the reason seemed to be concern for Grandma's emotional well being. After all, it was difficult enough for her to sleep in a strange place, much less bear the trauma of selling her home.

Perhaps I can come back with live-in help, she rationalized. None of us wanted to dash her hopes, though we knew it would never happen. One year later, Grandma now knows that she will never go back. Furthermore, the financial burden of maintaining two residences is causing as much stress as her physical ailments.

Maybe I can rent the house to my granddaughter Carrie, she proposed. When that plan fell through, she began to vocalize her desire to sell. "Bobby, you need to help clean out the house," she said to my dad. "David, you need to help do the repairs," she said to my uncle. So far, the only progress that's been made has come from one afternoon of cleaning by an eldercare worker and myself.

Why hasn't the family moved forward? I've asked myself that question many times. It could be that the amount of physical work ahead is daunting. Grandma was quite a saver; each room in the house is overflowing with possessions accumulated over 63 years. Cookware, clothing, magazines, medical records—all were saved because *you never know when you might need them*. I found prescription bottles dating back to 1968 in the hall closet.

As laborious as sorting, boxing, and hauling may be, the emotional tasks are more burdensome. Each physical object is imbued with a lifetime of memories. I've heard so many stories about my grandmother's wedding dress—how it came from Julie's, an upscale dress shop where she worked; how Aunt Alice played dress-up with it and left lipstick stains on the bodice; how it's stashed away in a trunk in the attic that no one has seen in 40 years. But even a seemingly insignificant item, such as a box of cake mix left in the cupboard, also brings back memories. I smile at the thought of Grandma's taking the same box of cake mix up north every summer, just in case someone felt like baking while on vacation. Yes, even now, I struggle with the notion that worldly goods are unimportant. Though I know I can always hold on to memories, I can't just dismiss all the personal affects of a life.

So what will the future hold for Grandma, and for the house on Toepfer Avenue? I ask myself that question every day. Someday, I know, the house will be sold—I'd like to imagine to a young couple just beginning their life together, as Grandma and Grandpa did some 64 years ago. I can't say I'm looking forward to that day, and neither are the other family members. I'm sure they would be grateful if I would spearhead the effort to clean out the house, but I just can't bring myself to do it. First of all, I strongly believe that the burden should not fall on just one person; this needs to be a joint effort. But beyond the practical concerns, my emotional issues still prevent me from taking action.

Some would say I'm in denial, unwilling to face the reality of life without my grandmother. Of course! Who wants to think about living without a person who loves you not because of what you do, but simply because you exist?

Some would say I'm living in the past, unable to let go of my childhood. Perhaps. However, my past grounds me in the present, with each decision I make shaped by a lifetime of experiences with my family.

Like Anne Bradstreet, I have been fortunate to lead a life that I love, a life that I have shared with my grandmother. But am I willing to forgo her worldly possessions? Not yet. Am I ready to let go of my grandmother? Not ever. She is my hope and treasure, to which I never want to say farewell.

Chapter 10

Liz Kozek

Grandpa's Cottage

Musty wood paneling
Picture window
Streaming July sunset.
Rippling lake below,
Gulls soar and swoop in shadowy relief.

Mounted game
Pictures of an angler who no longer walks the earth.
UNO cards abandoned on the table
And gritty floor that will not be swept clean of the beach's offerings.

Pine needles and sand
Shift underfoot
Nature's glorious "lights out" for the night
Ritual bonfire under heaven's bright stars.

Sanctuary.
History.
The cradle of our family.
And the enduring gift of our beloved patriarch.

A Mystery

Pickle day? How the hell did I come to this? Pickle day. Knocking on my door, I'm thirty years old and he wants to make pickles at eight in the morning? I understand he was trying to help and all, but pickle day? Lord, help me. I may lose my mind over this divorce if I have to put up with lunatic creations like Dad's "Pickle Day" to keep me occupied. But he will not be put off. So pickles will be made. To keep him happy. It's just such a pain in my ass ...

"Yee-oww! Shit, dude, that hurts!"

"It's seven needles burning black ink into your skin; it's gonna hurt," replies the deranged Santa Claus currently wielding his device of torture over my backside.

"Yeah, but give a girl a break, puh-leeze."

It's nearly Christmas Eve and I'm sitting in a tattoo parlor with my former high school English teacher, Daryl, who is currently my co-worker, and who is also snapping pictures of my lower backside while I try to figure out how I got into this position. It seemed like such a natural idea after holiday shopping and a meal of Pad Thai. Now I'm not so sure that coming to Peter Chistle and his den of horror was the best way to kill an afternoon.

"Here, read to me while I work. It'll take your mind off the pain."

A children's book is shoved into my hands, which are trapped between my knees as I'm doubled over with my shirt tucked into my bra with my pants hauled down to the crack of my ass, on display for everyone, including the Ansel Adams English teacher.

A children's book. A book about math, in fact. My least favorite subject. My now ex-husband's favorite subject. Dumbshit that he is, he thought I couldn't count high enough to figure out that his little *chica* was pregnant with their *bambino* l-o-o-o-ng before our divorce went through.

At least I got one last dig in. Why the hell would anyone willingly name their child Russell? That kid is gonna get pummeled on the playground. But reminding him about our buddy, who nick-named his penis "Russell-the-One-Eyed-

Muscle," will hopefully always be in the back of his mind every time the ex calls his son's name. Now there's a gift that keeps on giving!

Damn, that thing hurts. Seven needles carving ink into my skin? Why am I doing this again? Oh, that's right, because I need to maintain my track record of terrible decision making. I should've known when I was greeted at the door by an emaciated man dressed in a Santa hat and beard, and looking like a heroin-addicted Father Christmas in the Macy's Thanksgiving Parade, that I was not using my best judgment. And the "Starfucks" apron, that's a nice touch. Real classy. Almost as classy as the drawing of the cat with an open hole where his dick used to be with the title "Spayed" underneath. Why didn't I get *that* tattooed on my butt?

"This might be one of my better works," I hear over my shoulder.

I am reminded of the cat and I shudder.

Keep your mind on the artwork, Leonardo. I glance at the mirror that reflects the double reflection of Peter the Insane Santa, crouching over my backside, adding more detail to his creation.

This is making me tougher. Not only do I feel tougher, I'm gonna look tougher with my bad-ass tattoo. People won't kick me around like they did before. This is the new-and-improved Liz. Not the one who gets stalked by former pro-basketball players bearing doughnuts and pumpkins at parent-teacher conferences. Or the Liz who wiped up in the school's Holiday Canned Food Drive only to be disqualified for trading extra credit for cans. Or the Liz who threw up backstage before each performance of *A Few Good Men*. I can see by my reflection in this mirror that I won't get pushed around after this.

"Hey, keep reading."

Dutifully I continue to read. This time a different book. Why are these kids hopping on their father? Shouldn't he do something about it? What kind of destruction is Dr. Seuss promoting here? No wonder kids are so disrespectful. Like last week when Chris went back to school after our play and told everyone how he got to see my tits while I was changing backstage. Stellar casting decision, putting a high school student in a community theater production of play based on an R-rated movie. Just what I need. I bet the administration loved that one. I have to remember to talk to Chris about theater protocol and professionalism. This just won't do.

"Are you done yet?"

"Just finished the black outline. Now I'm switching to the color. This is going to require *nine* needles, so it may hurt a little bit more."

It's officially a toss up. I thought that I knew what pain was, but now I'm not so sure. When that doctor carved off the cancerous mass while I was in another similarly prone position (perhaps less modest than the one I am currently in since it required stirrups), I thought that I would never again experience anything that hurt so badly, short of childbirth. But I might be wrong about that now. This may, in fact, hurt more than childbirth.

"How much longer?"

"Just keep reading."

I look in the mirror across from me, but I don't want to watch the blood and ink smearing together across my tailbone. So I focus on my face. My eyes. Are those crow's feet? Do I look thirty years old? Turning thirty sucked. It probably didn't help that the entire student body sang "Happy Birthday" to me while I was trying to concentrate on dribbling a basketball in the student-staff basketball game. That's probably why I got distracted and clobbered that kid, knocking him to the ground. I don't understand basketball.

In fact, I don't understand sports in general. Why is it that I had to get dragged to all of those stupid Michigan football games? Getting up at four a.m. to bake cheesy potatoes for those incessant tailgates after a week of grad school and teaching. What was I getting, maybe three hours of sleep a night? And for what? The opportunity for *that man* to socialize with some undergrad who is now nursing his firstborn child? And in return for my hard work?

I now have a Master's Degree that has precluded me from spousal support from a man who makes three times what I do. Yeah, that's justice.

"Hey, Liz, lean to the side a little more so that I can get the right lighting. Jeez, you're bleeding like a hemophiliac back here!" followed by the click of the camera's shutter.

This I certainly don't need to know.

Did I ask this guy if he's using clean needles? Can I get The HIV from this? Not that it's gonna matter. I won't be a threat to public health. Not if I'm dating a guy who cries and prays for forgiveness after every orgasm. That's enough to put anybody off of dating. And Catholicism, too. Which is the bigger sin? Being divorced or having sex out of wedlock? What about having sex out of wedlock with a divorcee? I bet that it'd make him cry even harder if he knew.

"What colors do you want?"

"Surprise me."

Why not? Everything else is always a great big mystery. Like why is it that it's been my job to counsel everyone else through my own damn divorce? Everyone acts like it's some huge loss to *them*. Does anyone worry about how I'm feeling? Divorcing a hirsute, obese, and nearly toothless engineer doesn't seem like a big deal on paper, but if they want to treat it like it's a loss, go right ahead. Just leave me outta it. I'll take the crying Jesus-freak any day.

"Do you want pink or red tongues?"

Pink or red tongues? Since when did tongues enter into this equation? I don't remember giving any permission for tongues to be drawn on my ass. But since tongues *have* been drawn on my ass, what color should they be?

"Red."

To go with my hair. When am I going to change that? Am I a bigger bad-ass as a redhead or as a towhead? Maybe I could dye my hair to match the tattoo. I can do anything now! Maybe I'll go talk to that guy who's been stabbing girls' navels with big needles in the next stall, and get some kind of piercing. Maybe my eyebrow. Maybe my tongue. Hey, maybe *the tongue on my ass*!

"Nearly there. Just gotta stop the bleeding. I'm gonna lubricate it."

Why does this whole thing suddenly sound like a porn movie? It practically *is* a porn movie with Daryl snapping pictures of my butt-crack for the last two hours. I need to speak with him about making sure these don't get posted on the Internet. I'm not sure that my reputation can take another scandal.

Man, trouble just *finds* me.

Or do I find trouble? I don't know, it's a mystery.

Damn, I love that movie *Shakespeare in Love*. That's a good line. I'm going to use it more often: *I don't know, it's a mystery.* I'm going to find a way to work that into casual conversation.

"All right, what do you think?"

Oh-my-God. What the hell is *that*? I thought this thing was going to be the size of my big toe. How come it's as large as my hand? And are those tongues florescent pink? What happened to red? Purple and turquoise? That's what he chose?

"Umm, wow. It's great." How do I get it off? What was I thinking? I'm totally going to get tossed out of the family when they see these two psychotic faces with bright pink tongues and red eyes glaring back at them! Maybe no one will know. Maybe I can get it lasered off. Maybe I can get a discount because he got the eyes confused with the tongues.

No. This is the new bad-ass Liz. This is cool. You're cool now because you've endured your rite of passage with the grinning Satanic Santa. It's like life. Sometimes it throws a little pain in your path and you have to endure it, and you come out of it stronger. Remember? That's why you chose the masks of comedy and tragedy to be emblazoned on your backside. Two sides of the coin. The funny and the sad. The yin and the yang. The good and the bad. Sometimes it isn't what you had in mind when you set out, but you're stuck with it.

I mull this over as we leave Santa's lair of skin mutilation.

"So, what do you want to do next?"

"*I don't know. It's a mystery.*"

Grandpa's Cottage–Revisited in Prose

The sound of water in motion has always reminded me of my family's cottage on Lake Michigan. My grandfather, my mother's father, bought the tiny asbestos-shingled building in the summer of my birth, some 30 years ago.

The sound of the Great Lake's waves alternately lapping or crashing was omnipresent in all that we did. My sister and I would splash in the often-frigid water, despite the shivering and blue lips that such frolicking produced. The waves would slap against the sides of our boat as we fished for Lake Perch or King Salmon. The sound and the waves would ebb and flow as we stood in front of the cabin for the requisite Polaroid of our prize catch of the day, even if it were only one small Bluegill. The water's dance would continue as we stood by, enraptured, watching Grandpa skillfully disembowel our catch as part of the suppertime ritual.

The sound of moving water was always there, to lull our family to sleep, or sing to us at mealtimes, the cabin doors flung wide open to embrace its song.

Thirty-one years of a sound and sight, that was our companion. After leaving the cabin to come home, we always felt as if something were missing, something "just not right." It was the absence of the lake.

We are now older, some of us at the beginning of our careers while our parents have ended theirs, and the cottage is vacant more and more often as life's daily encumbrances prevent us from visiting. The man who bought that little place on the lake has since passed, and with his passing, seems to have taken with him the glue that bound us as a family, and to that hallowed cabin on the lake.

I go there alone now, any chance I can get. I drive the four hours in gridlocked traffic to park in the sandy, pine needle-laden excuse for a driveway; streak to the front of the cabin in the hopes of catching the last lights of a streaming sunset between the branches of trees; and listen to the sounds of the waves, pounding on the beach below.

I miss my grandfather the most at those moments, but I never feel more close to him than I do when I stand there, looking across the water.

Chapter 11

Lois Little

Gentle Purple Flower

Gentle purple flower,
Though I know you are a weed,
Help me pass this hour,
If in my garden you would seed.

Not the garden of my flowers,
But the garden of my mind,
Where we can while away the hours
Learning how to rhyme.

Briers to Butterflies: Inspired by Seven Words

A quill dipped in anger created a wave of fear,
Until the allegiance of love and friendship
Resonated across the expanse of time.

The El

    Elevated transit has always been my idea of what is the most exciting kind of mass transportation. Perhaps being born on the South Side of Chicago near the end of the 1940's has had something to do with it. The street car and the El have carried me to the Loop to see Santa, Shed's Aquarium, the Field Museum, the Art Institute and countless other exciting destinations.

Elevated trains are special because they carry you above the crowds and fumes of humanity; they give you a peek into the higher levels of the city. Now, I wonder, will I still be able to enjoy the city passing by, or will I be too occupied scrutinizing my fellow passengers and searching for abandoned packages.

Persevere: An Alphabet Poem

Alas, bravely climb:
Don't ever forget gravity.
Harbor interests.
Justify knowledge.
Live moments.
Negotiate opportunities.
Plan quests.
Rise, soar to untarnished visions.
Wander Xanadu, your zenith.

Pyromaniac

Education is not filling a bucket, but lighting a fire.
-William Butler Yates

Oh to be a pyromaniac and to light fires in the minds all my students. For as a fire consumes fuel, we want our children to consume knowledge. It is true that you can teach a student how to learn, and learn how to teach a student, but learning is the internal combustion that shines in our students' eyes and carries them forward to success.

Sometimes, it seems as if the fuel is too wet to catch the spark and ignite learning; it just smokes and sputters. Sometimes, the Regimental Administrative Fire Department seems to douse the flames with requirements and regulations. Yet how glorious it is, when we see that spark ignite and explode into a roaring inferno before our eyes. Yes, I love being a flint!

A Home for Max–A Friend for Sam

A home for Max! I'll give him a home:
Out on the street, where the strays have to roam.

How dare they think I need a friend?
This "friend" might send me around the bend!

I know he's there behind the door;
When it is quiet, I hear him snore.

Good grief he is big! I hope he is gentle.
If I wanted a "friend," I would have called Yentl.

I am Sam; I rule this house.
Sam I am; don't you dare grouse.

I hiss and growl; I look into his eyes.
He looks away; at least he's wise.

He doesn't like catnip, which is strange but fine;
It just means that all these new toys now are mine.

He drools, he begs, he comes when they call;
I wonder if he's a cat at all.

When we play tag, I always win;
I know the places he can't fit in.

Time has shown he's not a bad fellow;
Sometimes I let him share my pillow.

He's not so bad, this cat called Max;
Though there are days, my nerves he'll tax.

All right, all right! I like having Max as a friend;
He brings long days to a quicker end.

What is that? Do I smell fish?

Back off Max; that's still my dish!

A Teacher of the Soul

I knew I would be late for school, but I couldn't help it. I quickly pulled the car to the side of the road, tears pouring from my eyes as I grabbed the shovel from the trunk of the car. Slowly I scooped Charlie off the smooth wet pavement and placed him gingerly in the back. I drove home sobbing; the excruciating loss was almost more than I could bear. As I pulled into the driveway, a gray furry blur jumped into the front picture window. I gasped and couldn't believe my eyes; if that was Charlie, who was in my trunk?

I'd been in a hurry that morning, and somehow I had missed seeing my cat, Charlie. Under pressure, my mind had jumped to the conclusion that he had gotten out and been hit by a car. Had my mind been working rationally, I would have realized that I was too far from the house for the victim to be Charlie; but, as is so often the case with animals and children, my mind was not working rationally. I don't usually bury random road kill in my back yard, but I just couldn't put Charlie's twin back on the side of the road to rot.

Yes, I am one of those animal lovers. People often think I'm a little crazy; I know they are wrong. Animals bring something special to our lives. They awaken a special place in our hearts, teaching us about unconditional love, faithfulness, trust, loss, compassion, and much, much more. All they ask for in return is to be near us, to protect us, to listen to us, and to share some of what we have.

I have been blessed with several great "teachers of the soul," both dogs and cats, each with their own lessons to share. Bobo, the Boxer of my childhood, taught me patience and loyalty. Oden, the destructive Dalmatian, taught me to forgive, while Sandy, our Golden Retriever, showed me how to grow old with courage and dignity. Dozo, the little Japanese cat, rescued us from rats and demonstrated a mother's love and patience. Charlie, her son, was the only cat we raised from a kitten. He was very dear to my heart, teaching me to have faith and to never give up. Charlie showed me how to ask for help and then accept it. Next came Yancy and Emmy Sue; stray cats rescued by my sister and passed on to me. Their lessons of charity and gratitude have made me a better person. Now, I am fortunate to live with Sam and Max. Sam has taught me you can find compassion in the most unlikely places, if you will only give it a chance to shine. As for Max, well Max is Max; a delightful bundle of contradictions and surprises.

Max began as a surprise. The night that my daughter Sarah and I made a quick stop at PetSmart for cat food was not supposed to be the beginning of a feline love affair. On a whim, I suggested we take a look at the cats. It was love at first sight. Max lay sprawled across the front of his cage, his head resting on his turbo ball. He looked so forlorn; I just had to hold him. Sarah knew I was smitten, but she had some doubts. We had talked about finding a friend for Sam, someone to take the place of her littermate, Jim, but we were still in the speculation stage. Sam had been alone since my daughter had moved home and her friend Dee had taken Jim to her new apartment. Sarah wanted Sam to be happy and have a friend to keep her company during the day, but she was worried about her diminutive kitten's safety.

Normally, I am not impulsive, especially when it comes to important events and decisions. Experience has taught me to think about consequences and priorities before I act, but with Max I couldn't help myself. One pleading look from that big furry lover boy melted my heart. His big white paws reached out through the cage as I reached in to rub him under the chin. The card on his cage announced that his name was Max; he was four years old and good with other cats. Sarah couldn't believe that I was serious, but went to get an employee to take Max from his cage. Once freed, he rolled over on his back, purred, and kneaded the air with his big white paws. His whole tummy and all four legs were as white as snow, a fact we wear on our dark clothes every day. Sarah had worked for a veterinarian and commented that Max's trusting manner was a good sign. The truth was that he had won her over too.

Jill, the PetSmart employee, told us that Max was a great cat and that all of the staff loved him. She also explained that we would have to apply to the rescue agency to adopt Max, and if we were approved, there would be a one hundred dollar fee. Sarah and I agreed that he was worth it and filled out the paperwork, laughing when they asked where he would sleep. "Anywhere he wants," I replied, "just like all the other cats we've had." Later that week, we brought Max home, along with a carload of cat toys and accoutrements.

The rescue agency suggested that we keep Max and Sam separated for several weeks, but that idea only lasted several days. Both cats had previously lived with other cats, so we decided to take a chance. Sam immediately took the upper hand and still maintains control, to one degree or another. Max is just his laid back self. He usually yields to Sam and does his own thing, except when he wants to play. Then he hisses, growls, and "Thunder Cats" can be heard tearing through the house. I'm not sure what kind of cats Gilbert and Sullivan had, but trust me when I say that we have no "cat-like tread" stealing up on us around here!

Max is at home now and has brought much humor into our house. He seems to instinctively know when we need a good laugh and is determined to be accepted as an Alpha Phi Omega fraternity brother, inserting himself into section staff meetings and sitting on agendas. He is affectionate and great company when we want it and even when we don't. My son is convinced that Max is the perfect pet, a dog in a cat's body. Like most dogs, Max is loyal and friendly. He loves being with people, and has thrown himself against the sliding glass door in an attempt to join my daughter and her friends on the porch and the patio. Max walks in a harness, begs for food, snores, farts, and cleans his dish, never nibbling like a normal cat.

Cat or dog, it doesn't matter. Max's gentle persistence has won over all of us, even Sam. Every day, Max demonstrates that you don't have to dominate as long as you stay true to yourself. Like the Sun, when it defeated the Wind, Max teaches that gentle, patient persistence accomplishes far more than angry brute force. I am thankful that Max found his home with us. He is a great teacher of the soul, never discouraged, coming back again and again with a gentle nudge or rub until he succeeds in his quest.

Chapter 12

Herman A. Peterson

Hello, My Name Is …

My name is Herman,
but that is not the name my mother gave me.
It means "man of war"
in German.
Tenacity and struggle
invade my life.

My name is Herman,
but that is not the name my mother gave me.
When I left the monastery
after nine years
I kept the name I took as a monk.
Religion remains
central in my life.

My name is Herman,
but that is not the name my mother gave me.

A sainted eleventh century monk
crippled by polio,
he was a mathematician, astronomer, composer—
the Stephen Hawking of his age.
Overcoming adversity
inspires my life.

My name is Herman,
but that is not the name my mother gave me.
The name my mother gave me was
Adam, now my second name.
The name God gave me is first
in my life.

The Face of the Child

When Moses asked to see God's face
He was refused this singular grace.
Man cannot see the face of God and live.

And yet this same too Holy face
Appeared for us on earth encased
In human flesh, our life to live.

The tetrarch tried to pierce the face
Of every child born in that place—
Dispose of God that he might live.

God's earthly father saved the face
Of heaven's Child from such disgrace,
For we must see the face of God to live.

a Sabbath afternoon

too long sleeping
sheet-creased lingering
neck pain waking
groggy moving
too long persisting

too cold raining
grayness weighing
redundant napping
interest absenting
motivation thwarting
too cold eating

Creator resting
man attempting

Marathon to Galloway Creek

Blackbirds,
Butterflies,
and Blackberries.

Chickadees,
Chicory,
and Chokecherries.

Gravel,
Grasshoppers,
and Grapes.

Sounds,
Sights,
and Succulence.

Reservation Remote

 Somehow I got control of the remote, which is always a mistake when I'm in the mood to talk instead of watch TV. As my roommate, Martin, sat down cross-legged on his recliner, he gave me a sidelong glance. I clicked on the TV to find it tuned to *Animal Planet* and some show about dogs.

 "Martin," I said, "you remember the dogs on the rez?" He nodded absently.

 "I remember when I first visited your mother's house on the rez. I was struck by how many dogs were running around outside. Every one of the neighbors seemed to have at least six mutts. Some were friendly. Some were beautiful. Some weren't either. But they *all* seemed to be hungry *all* the time. At first I thought that none of them was being taken care of, but then as I spent more time there looking at those dogs I came to realize that most of them were well-beloved pets. Sure, they didn't look like the dogs in the suburbs and they weren't cared for in the same way as dogs in the suburbs, but they were loved nonetheless. Do you remember that?"

Martin ran his hand through his short black hair and grunted as I flipped through the channels. I came to rest on the news where the anchor was saying something about the Bush administration.

"Martin," I said, "you remember when Bush appointed 'Famous' Dave Anderson as the head of the Bureau of Indian Affairs?"

"I remember the ribs and fries at his restaurant. They were really tasty even before his chain went national."

"I remember the powwow they had for him before he went to Washington. You didn't want to come that day, did you? They had a pipe ceremony to open it and they kept giving him gifts. Someone gave him a quilt, another group gave him an eagle feather, the Tribe gave him a pipe—I think—and someone gave him a beautifully beaded pipe bag. Each time he received a gift he danced around the school gym with it, accompanied by his family and the people who gave the gift. It was a beautiful afternoon. His restaurant had the best booze in town too, didn't it?"

"Now *that* I remember."

I continued clicking absentmindedly through the channels until I came to a Budweiser commercial.

"Martin," I said, "you remember when I was unemployed for so long I didn't have any money left for whiskey, or anything else for that matter?"

"Sure."

"I remember I worked for your grandmother for awhile. She asked me if I had ever worked with concrete. I said that when I was a kid I helped my dad lay the foundation for his cabin, but that was ... She interrupted me in mid-sentence and told me she wanted me to lay a concrete slab for her at the entrance to the back door. After I explained all the advantages of hiring a professional for such work, she said she wanted me to try. So I did and it turned out all right, didn't it?"

"Yeah, but the brick patio you laid for her the next week has more waves than Lake Superior."

"But we sure got drunk off the money I made, didn't we?"

"I guess. Can we watch something else?"

"Sorry."

The next channel had a movie about the Navajo code talkers during World War II. One of them was showing a photograph of his family. His wife was wearing some beautifully handcrafted jewelry in turquoise and silver.

"Martin," I said, "you remember those bags I made for your grandmother?"

"What about them?"

"I remember doing a lot of beadwork at your mother's house. Every day, it seemed, I was doing beadwork. When your grandmother saw some of it, she never said she was impressed or that she liked it. She just asked me to make four beaded bags for her that she needed for a giveaway. One I made out of buckskin that she gave me, but the other three were cloth. She didn't like the cloth ones at first. She wanted shoulder straps rather than handles. It would have helped if she had told me that ahead of time. I was really proud of the way those bags turned out, and I felt honored that she would ask an overweight, middle-aged, unemployed white guy like me to make them for her. Do you remember those bags?"

"We used that money for whiskey too, didn't we?"

"I'm sure we did. We were both drinking pretty heavily then."

"I remember the time your car was stuck in the mud."

"Yeah, you had gone out the night before and didn't come home until morning. I woke you up and asked you where my car was. I had to get really angry with you before you would get up and give me an answer. You just remembered waking up in the passenger seat of the car on a dirt road. It was stuck in the mud and you walked home."

Martin was chuckling. "When you first came to the rez your car was real nice, but after I pulled off the bumper trying to get it out of that snow bank, it was never the same. It got 'rezified.'" Laughing in the face of misfortune was a typical reaction for Martin. I just sat there pensively.

The next channel that caught my eye was airing an episode of a mini-series. The scene showed an Indian and a crooked white trader. The Indian wanted to trade for guns to protect his family from a hostile neighboring tribe, but the trader talked the Indian into accepting whiskey instead, thirsting for them to become addicted.

"Martin," I said, "you remember your friend Tauri?" Martin just started absently bouncing his foot.

"I remember driving around with Tauri on the rez one day. I guess you were too hung-over to come. We were looking for weed and she was telling me about all the troubles in her family. That was one messed up family. Then all of a sudden we saw a bald eagle swoop down over the road directly in front of us. She screamed at me to stop the car, so I did. We both put tobacco down near the place where we had seen the eagle. She explained that seeing an eagle was a sign that the Creator had heard your prayer–that everything would turn out okay. Placing sacred tobacco on the ground was a way to show gratitude. I told her that I had been worrying about getting a job and the bad financial situation I was in. She told me more stories about her family."

"That was good weed, too."

"I wouldn't know," I said. "A few days after that Tauri came over to the house late at night. She was all bloody and crying. Her older brother had beaten her up pretty badly. I was furious. I couldn't believe it, but she forgave him a couple days later. I still don't understand how she could have forgiven him that easily."

"Just change the channel."

There was an old John Wayne western on the next channel. He was leading the Cavalry in a charge over the hill to rescue some white woman from the Indians.

"Martin," I said, "you remember your cousin Adam's graduation? He was really proud of his achievement."

Martin adjusted his T-shirt and didn't say a word.

"I remember that he went to the school on the rez, not to the high school in town where your sister went. It was in the school gym. I remember lots of milling about and low mumblings and nods of greeting. After most people moseyed to their seats, the drum began to beat and the high-pitched honor song rang out. We all stood as the green-clad graduands entered the hall in caps and gowns with fluttering eagle feathers instead of tassels. After the ceremony we all gathered at your grandmother's house. She was on the phone ordering pizza and then asked me if I would drive into town to pick it up. On the way I noticed that I needed gas, so I stopped for a fill-up. Between the gas station and the bait shop next door, a mother bear and her two cubs were up in a tree. I knew then for sure that it was a good day for a celebration.

"I remember that Adam received a gift of fifty dollars from the tribe. The next day he gave me some gas money to take him into town. We went to Wal-Mart. He bought a game for his PlayStation and a lot more chocolate than was good for his complexion. On the way home we stopped for a twenty-bag, and his money was gone."

"Do you remember that?"

Martin grabbed the remote out of my hand. "Just shut up and let me watch TV."

All I could do was sigh.

Letters to Sherman Alexie: Deluded, Disillusioned, Delighted

23rd June 2003

Dear Mr. Alexie:

Recently, I had the opportunity to see your movie *The Business of Fancydancing*. One line in particular captured my attention; you state that life on a Native American reservation is "equal parts magic and loss." What did you mean by that?

My opinion is …

The Native life is more resplendent still
With beadwork, buckskin, trade cloth, ribbon frill.

The Native life is more harmonious still
With coursing beats of drums and voices shrill.

The Native life is more delicious still
With berries, fish, and deer the cravings fill.

The Native life is more sweet-scented still
With sweet grass, sage, tobacco—smoky thrill.

The Native life is more kinetic still
With dancers lost in grace, replete with skill.

The Native life is more connected still
To birds and beasts, to feather, fur, and gill.

This "loss" you speak, I know it not,
But "magic" marks the perfect spot.

Sincerely,
Herman A. Peterson, D.Min.

October 14, 2003

Dear Sherman,

Visited reservation.

Saw "loss."

no economy	just theft
no tomorrow	just beer
no hope	just crack
no conversation	just cursing
	complaining
	conniving
no culture	just slots
no art	just Cable
no imagination	just rage
no silence	just breaking
	beating
	bellowing

Yours truly,
Herman Peterson

4/24/04

Sherm,

I found a refuge on the rez
      Asylum while unemployed
           Fostered friend in a flock of family.

Cousins like canned commodities
      At every meal.

Aunties like anthills
      In all directions.

An extra neighbor
> In unexpected rooms.

Six siblings each
> Or so it seems.

One Grandma
> Omnipresent.

Each has chosen magic.
> Loss has chosen each.

They coincide like a quilt
> And embrace me like my blanket.

Now,
> Only now,
>> Do I get it.

Later,
Herm

A Powerful Essay:
Contra Pelagiani or What Exactly is a Bootstrap Anyway?

"Hi, I'm Herman and I'm an alcoholic." That's what I say before I share some part of my story at an AA (Alcoholics Anonymous) meeting. Alcoholism is a disease, and publicly identifying myself as someone who suffers from this disease is an attempt on my part to own my powerlessness over it. This is the very first step in recovering from alcoholism: "We admitted we were powerless over alcohol–that our lives had become unmanageable."

Powerlessness is not an easy thing to admit, but paradoxically that is exactly what an alcoholic needs to do if he or she wants to quit drinking. Alcoholism is not simply a matter of lack of will power, though some still think that way. Power and will are exactly what an alcoholic needs to give up in order to put the disease into remission. Very often the most difficult part of recovery from alcoholism is dealing with the shame involved in the admission of powerlessness. But why should there be shame involved? There *is* shame involved—that much is clear from the experience of thousands of recovering alcoholics.

It seems to me that shame is always culturally conditioned to some extent because it involves how a person feels in the presence of others. I am not ashamed to be naked in the shower, but I would be ashamed to be naked in public. The acceptability of public nudity varies from culture to culture. If, then, shame is culturally conditioned, why is there shame involved in the public admission of powerlessness in our culture? Sometimes it's easier to gain insights into your own culture by comparing it to another.

Many Native American spiritual traditions have a much different philosophy on the nature of human will and power. All created things possess will, not only humans and sentient animals but trees, rocks, winds, and storms. The conception of will finds its model in the unpredictable will of a storm or a mountain stream. This is very different from the conception of will in Euro-American philosophy and takes a moment to absorb. A hurricane, for example, has a will of its own. Human will, therefore, is something like the vagaries of a hurricane.

Power, especially power over will, is something that always comes from the spiritual realm. If you want protection from the will of the hurricane, you pray. The answer to your prayer is dependent on your relationship with the spiritual, something that must be maintained on a regular basis so that prayers in time of need will be acted upon. Analogously, if you want power over your own will, you pray and maintain your relationship to the spiritual. This is essentially the whole idea behind the AA program.

So, why then are so many Native Americans practicing alcoholics? Aside from their hereditary predisposition toward this disease, it must be remembered that their culture and language were stolen from them in a very systematic fashion. Euro-Americans called it "Manifest Destiny" and correctly saw Native American spiritual ideas as inimical to the advance of capitalism and the Industrial Revolution.

The capitalist ideal, founded on the Protestant work ethic, is precisely the origin of the shame associated with powerlessness in Euro-American culture. The German philosopher Max Weber located the success of capitalism in the popularity of Protestant denominations based on the theology of John Calvin. Without confusing the issue with a mass of theological detail, it was Calvin's doctrine of predestination that led to the very practical insight that "God helps those who help themselves." Calvinism encourages this spirituality of self-reliance. On the individualism inherent in this principle was born all the great American ideas—not only liberty, freedom and opportunity, but also Manifest Destiny—and the treatment of Native Americans as subhuman that resulted from it.

Of course Calvin's theology speaks of God's grace, His power to assist human beings in guiding even their own wills. However, the feeling of shame that follows from powerlessness does not operate on the level of theology, but on the level of culture. Culture, it seems to me, is much more influenced by ideas of popular religiosity than by ideas of theology. Popular religiosity does not always have room for the delicate distinctions of theology. So, Euro-American culture has absorbed and enshrined Calvin's notion of individualism without paying much attention to his notion of grace. "God helps those who help themselves" is the maxim adopted by the culture.

Just to be ecumenically fair, even Catholics who immigrated to this country were highly influenced by Calvin through the vehicle of the culture they found here. The American dream had a powerful effect on the level of popular religiosity for Catholics. Rather than accusing them of Calvinism, however, it might be more politically correct to call them unwitting Pelagians. Pelagius was a monk who thrived around the turn of the fifth century. The heresy attributed to him is that human beings are capable, through their own merit and without the help of God's grace, to earn salvation. This, of course, is the ultimate "pull yourself up by your own bootstraps" theology.

Think about that image for a moment. A person has fallen down and is trying to get back up by pulling on the straps attached to his own boots. It's a comedy routine worthy of the Three Stooges—and that's precisely the point. No one can pull himself or herself up that way, and it's ridiculous to expect it. But our culture teaches us to expect it anyway. This is the difficulty with feeling ashamed about powerlessness, that in this instance, our culture expects us to accomplish the manifestly absurd.

I am an alcoholic, and I am *not* ashamed to admit that I suffer from a disease, even though my culture encourages that reaction. I value my freedom as an American and am very grateful to live in this "land of opportunity," but that does not mean that I need to swallow the rampant individualism that is promoted by my culture. My continuing recovery from alcoholism depends on my Higher Power rather than my own bootstraps.

Further Reading

Alcoholics Anonymous. 4th ed. New York: AA World Services, 2001.

Kidwell, Clara Sue, Homer Noley, and George E. "Tink" Tinker. *A Native American Theology.* Maryknoll, NY: Orbis Books, 2001.

Rees, B.R. *Pelagius: A Reluctant Heretic.* Woodbridge, Suffolk: The Boydell Press, 1988.

Twelve Steps and Twelve Traditions. New York: AA World Services, 1981.

Weber, Max. *The Protestant Ethic and the Spirit of Capitalism.* New York: Charles Scribner's Sons, 1958.

Chapter 13

Kathleen Reddy-Butkovich

What Gives?

To be literate is to listen, to observe intently,
see what the moment gives and ask, "What does it mean?"
-from my notes at a Donald Graves lecture UNH, 1987

I keep that definition in my "back pocket." It's next to the poems. It's right there with my father's advice during driver's training: Drive by the seat of your pants. Know the manuals and the safety rules, but when you're driving, feel the road. Be aware of your passenger's comfort. Think about the confidence they must have in you, just to get in the car.

So what does a pocket inventory have to do with good teaching? Well, I tried to put the state mandates, new curriculum guides, and the school district's view of parents and students as customers into that pocket. Then I added the forms for how to get new stuff for the classroom and the directions for how to use all the new stuff. To this, I carefully added the remote control for the classroom TV monitor, telephone, and the computer connections, state-of-the-art stuff.

On top of that, a stack of teacher-store catalogs arrived filled with teacher-proof, prepared lessons and cute projects for every grade level and Hallmark Card holiday. When I tried to tuck those into my "back pocket," right next to a new classroom seating chart for thirty desks and a door key ... it just didn't sit right! So it's time to empty that pocket and decide what to keep close at hand.

I'm going to keep the Donald Graves quotation. I will use it as my personal curriculum guide. It values listening, observing, and asking questions to reach new levels of understanding. It allows me to be a thinking reader, writer, and professional educator. It supports decision-making. I want that in my life and in my teaching and for my students. The poems stay. They speak to the heart in all of this and will continue to be my best resource.

I'm going to think of students and their parents, not as customers, but as *passengers*. Teaching is not about building cars or selling a product. Perhaps it is about driver's training. It's about where we are going and if the passengers have the confidence to get into the car. I need to get back into the driver's seat. I know the stuff in the manuals. I know how kids learn. I miss the feel of the road.

I'm going to stop running teaching errands, turning around and telling the passengers to "cut it out back there." We have a challenging journey. We will look out the windows together, notice places for learning, plan our stops along the way, and enjoy the rhythm of the ride. Now more than ever, I need to drive by the seat of my pants. I am aware of my passenger's comfort and that this road, each student's education, is still under construction. This is no time to lose my grip on the wheel!

Well, maybe one more errand ... I'm going to use the catalogs and order some more blank paper and a new box of markers. I think I'll fax the order.

When's Recess? *

Friendship is a seesaw:
With ups and downs,
Weighty points of balance,
Needing the other to rise.

The ups and downs
Change point of view.
Needing the other to rise,
The game continues.

Change point of view–
Beyond determined roles.
The game continues;

The work shifts.

Weighty points of balance
Beyond determined roles
The work shifts;
Friendship is a seesaw.

A pantoum is a sixteen-line form with repeated lines or rhymes. Some sources agree that the pantoum in written form can be traced back to Malaysia and the 1400s.

Chapter 14

Stacy Tines

Holy Water

The healing water of the baptism by John.

The miracle water turned into wine for the wedding guests.

The calming water as He speaks to the masses aboard a fishing boat.

The refreshing water after forty days and forty nights.

The cleansing water washing the dirty feet of his followers.

The painful water to quench His thirst upon the cross.

The holy water bringing me into His kingdom.

Roaming Holiday

I'm going to Rome.

The plane touches down in a field.

The train speeds through the landscape.

Rick Steves proclaims, "Visit the three tiers of the crumbling Coliseum's wall."

My Catholic mother-in-law advocates, "Seek out the healing hands of Pope John Paul's communal blessings to all."

Fodors reads, "Seeing the radiant image of the pale blue ceiling of the Sistine Chapel is the thing to do."

Gregory Peck's character coaxes, "The Mouth of Truth.... put your hand in it." And you feel like you should too.

But instead, through Rome I tried to roam.

The haggard woman hangs wrinkled clothes from window frames.

Cousin Bruno sweeps us up in the history of our ancestors' names.

The scraggly kitten that scuttles over the ancient ruins looks meek.

Marcella gives warm kisses on your left and right cheek.

The train speeds through the landscape.

The plane takes off in a field.

I'm going to roam.

Voyage of the Heart

It smelled of body odor and cheap cologne, people, like sardines, packed uncomfortably close to one another. Women held tightly to their imitation Prada purses. Of the language floating throughout the space, "ciao," "si," "spaghetti," was all that we understood. As the crowd pushed everyone to the right, we moved with the masses, hoping this was our exit. When we looked back onto the subway, a man with a guilty smile looked back at us. My husband had just been pickpocketed.

This was to be the vacation of a lifetime. My husband and I had saved every last penny in a bank account labeled "*Vacation.*" It included pocket change, tutoring payments, and money not spent on movie rentals and fast food. Together with our travel companions and good friends, we poured over travel guides like, *Italy for Dummies.* We made reservations for an audience with the Pope, booked a tour of the City of the Dead beneath the Vatican, and made a "must see" list that included sites like the Pantheon, the Roman Forum, and Circus Maximus. If only we had known. You can't plan for everything, and in the end, you still end up feeling like "dummies" in Italy.

During our time in Rome, we stayed at the Gioia Bed and Breakfast. It sounds quaint, doesn't it? Our innkeeper spoke very little English, though she tried her best, knowing Americans adapt to new cultures so well. Though we understood very little, I did translate "your room" and "shitty." "What?" I giggled, when my husband and I were behind the closed bedroom door. After one night, we realized that "shitty" was the scent our room emitted.

One of our ventures outside Rome was to the ancient city of Pompeii. While there, we decided to climb Mt. Vesuvius. Little did we know that the journey to the volcano's base would be more of an adventure than the hike to its peak.

Stepping onto the tour bus with travelers from Germany, Italy, and America, we didn't know what we were getting into. Each of my rapid heartbeats corresponded with sharp turns of the wheel. The path looked as if it was made for a man on horseback, not for a bus driver with a 60-passenger bus. Being prone to motion sickness, I was close to losing it, but what do you do when stepping off the bus meant a 400 foot drop?

The final straw that sent me over the edge was when we passed another bus. After 15 minutes of reverse, forward, reverse, forward–we survived. The side view mirror and my nerves were the only causalities. I kissed the ground when we reached the volcano's base and contemplated walking the ten miles back to Pompeii, instead of taking my chances in the bus on the drive back.

One of the planned highlights of our trip was to visit my husband's grandfather's birthplace, Ciprano. We met his cousin Bruno at the subway station in the pouring rain, eager to travel the branches of our family tree. After an hour-and-a-half car ride, with a lot of talking but not much understanding, we reached our destination.

Ciprano is a small town with a river, where we imagined my husband's grandfather might have fished. We visited Hotel Ida, a local hot spot today, just as it had been 75 years ago. My husband snapped photos of the DeLuca family name, which was plastered throughout the town. The grand finale was seeing the DeLuca family homestead, now surrounded by a tall wire fence. As I posed my husband in front of his grandfather's home, I could see him pondering memories of his childhood.

Sadly, our happy thoughts were burst like a balloon when we reached home and shared our photos with my mother-in-law. This was not the same home that she had stood in front of six years ago on a similar tour.

Our final day in Rome—to no one's surprise—tested our patience once again. We met our travel partners at the bed and breakfast lobby at 7 am to catch our 8:15 am train to the airport. Little did we know that a quick stop for McDonald's would result in an 800-meter dash. And, if you know about track, the 800-meter is a run, not a "dash."

After a much longer-than-expected wait at the Roman Mickey D's, we realized that we were going to be late. The departure time board flashed, "AIRPORT 8:15." This meant our train was boarding! With carry-ons, wheeled suitcases, jackets in tow, and Egg McMuffins in hand, we were off. Being a former 800-meter runner, I took off in the lead. In *Home Alone* style, we hoofed it through the terminal. After covering what seemed like a marathon distance, we leapt onto the train stairwell and melted into the cushy seats to enjoy our well-deserved breakfasts, heart-attacks-in-a-sack

Though the vacation may not have been exactly what we planned, it was a vacation of a lifetime. Surprisingly, I've shared these stories more often than I have the ones about the breathtaking view from Mt. Vesuvius, the magnitude of St. Peter's Cathedral, or the best gnocchi I've ever tasted.

It's true that nothing is ever quite what you expect or imagine: Christmas morning, your first love, college, marriage, or even vacations. It's those unexpected moments that make memories out of mere, ordinary vacations. The greatest lesson is learning that all the planning in the world can't prepare you for a voyage of the heart.

978-0-595-46792-1
0-595-46792-X

Printed in the United States
91512LV00006B/49-66/A